ACCLA

DANCIN

D0615187

"Should be required reading for anyone hoping to understand the growing appeal of authoritarian leaders in Eastern Europe today . . . Combining black humor with lyrical prose, Szabłowski brilliantly captures the tragic disorientation of men and women whose lives were bifurcated by the sudden collapse of Communism and ruthless onslaught of neoliberal capitalism. . . . A poignant allegory about the human costs of regime change."

> —Kristen Ghodsee, author of *Red Hangover: Legacies of Twentieth-Century Communism*

"A fascinating and wide-ranging book that shows how, across different and diverse species, old habits die slowly, if at all. Humans, like other animals, often don't know when they've gained freedom because conditions of oppression have become the norm and they're unable to adjust to a newfound lack of restraint. Szabłowski's clever and metaphorical use of dancing bears to make this point is beautifully done."

> —Marc Bekoff, University of Colorado; coauthor of *The Animals' Agenda: Freedom, Compassion, and Coexistence in the Age of Humans*

"What a gem of a book. . . . So eloquent and original about the psychological transition from regimes."

> —Ruth Ben-Ghiat, New York University

"A brisk narrative [and] a surprising look at societies grappling with profound change." —*Kirkus Reviews*

"Heartrending . . . A sharply drawn account." —*Publishers Weekly*

PENGUIN BOOKS

DANCING BEARS

Witold Szabłowski is an award-winning Polish journalist. At age twenty-five he became the youngest reporter at the Polish daily newspaper *Gazeta Wyborcza*'s weekly supplement, *Duży Format*, where he covered international stories in countries including Cuba, South Africa, and Iceland. His features on the problem of illegal immigrants flocking to the EU won the European Parliament Journalism Prize; his reportage on the 1943 massacre of Poles in Ukraine won the Polish Press Agency's Ryszard Kapuściński Award; and his book about Turkey, *The Assassin from Apricot City*, won the Beata Pawlak Award and an English PEN award, and was nominated for the Nike Award, Poland's most prestigious literary prize. Szabłowski lives in Warsaw.

DANCING BEARS

BEARS

True Stories of People Nostalgic

for Life Under Tyranny

WITOLD SZABŁOWSKI

Translated by Antonia Lloyd-Jones

PENGUIN BOOKS

PENGUIN BOOKS

An imprint of Penguin Random House LLC
375 Hudson Street
New York, New York 10014
penguin.com

Originally published in Polish by Agora SA, Warsaw

Photos by Albin Biblom
Maps by Wawrzyniec Święcicki
All images courtesy of Agora SA

This publication has been supported by the © POLAND Translation Program.

ISBN 9780143129745
Ebook ISBN 9781101993385

CONTENTS

PART TWO

AUTHOR'S NOTE

Some of the names in this book have been changed to protect the privacy of individuals.

Athens: Every day thousands of Greeks here dream that one day their country will finally be run by the best and happiest system: Communism.

Belgrade: For many years war criminal Radovan Karadžić was here in hiding, disguised as a doctor of alternative medicine.

Berat: Here a construction worker, Djoni, smashes up the bunkers built by Enver Hoxha.

Gori: Here, in the house where Stalin was born, the generalissimo's death mask is guarded by his vestal virgins.

Havana: Thousands of Cubans tremble as they hear reports about the declining health of Fidel Castro, some in horror, others in hope that the winds of change will finally start to blow on their island too.

London: Lady Peron's five acres are located here, between the Victoria railway and coach stations.

Kosovska Mitrovica: Good friends Florent and Dušan set off from here to distribute chickens to the Serbs who come home to Kosovo.

Medyka: Day in and day out, thousands of "ants" walk across the Ukraine border here, bringing vodka and cigarettes into Poland.

Narva: The capital of the Estonian Russians, where not even the police can speak Estonian.

Sierakowo Sławieńskie: In the fight against poverty, the former residents of a state farm that was located here have founded the Hobbits' Village. They dress up as figures out of Tolkien and invite kids to take part in field games.

Tirana: Enver Hoxha ruled Albania from here, where there's still a pyramid designed in his memory by his daughter and son-in-law.

Belitsa: This town is the site of the thirty-acre Dancing Bears Park, where the bears are taught to live in freedom.

Dryanovets: This is the home of brothers Gyorgy and Stefan Marinov. Gyorgy used to travel the Black Sea coast and the local fairs with his female bear, Vela. Stefan was an expert in the extremely difficult art of wrestling with a bear.

Getsovo: Here, in 2007, the last three dancing bears in Bulgaria—Misho, Svetla, and Mima—were taken away from the Stanev family.

Yagoda: A town whose bear keepers were famous, though poorer than their colleagues in the north of the country. The Bulgarians used to say with a sneer that every resident of Yagoda had a bear at home.

Loznitsa: This village was the birthplace of Pencho Kubadinski, who hid with Gypsy bear keepers during the Second World War and later became one of the best known Bulgarian Communists—a close friend and colleague of Todor Zhivkov.

Sofia: Here in the capital city, only a few years ago, you could still see bear keepers in trams, at housing developments, and even outside stores or lottery-ticket sales outlets. They played the *gadulka*—a traditional string instrument—and begged for handouts.

Varna, Golden Sands: Not many years ago, before Bulgaria joined the European Union, the most popular Bulgarian resorts were still full of bear keepers and their animals.

INTRODUCTION

The guy with the wacky hair and the crazed look in his eyes did not appear out of nowhere. He was already known to them. Sometimes he said how great they were, and told them to go back to their roots; if need be, he threw in some highly unlikely but madly alluring conspiracy theory. Just to get them to listen. And to give them a fright. Because he'd noticed that if he scared them, they paid him more attention.

They'd gotten used to him being there, and to the fact that now and then, with a totally straight face, he said something unintentionally hilarious. Sometimes he hovered on the fringes of political life, sometimes closer to the mainstream, but he was generally regarded as a mild eccentric.

Until one fine day they rubbed their eyes in amazement. Because the guy with the wacky hair had entered the race for one of the highest offices in the land. And just as before, here he was, trying to scare them again—with talk of refugees, war, and unprecedented disaster. With anything at all. He was also trying to pump up the national ego. In the process—in the eyes of the so-called elite—he was making a bit of a fool of himself. But he was also making big promises. Above all, he promised to turn back time, and make things the way they used to be. In other words, better.

And he won.

You know where this happened? Yes, you're right. In our part of the world. In post-communist Central and Eastern Europe. In Regime-Change Land.

Regime-Change Land is the lava that began to pour from the volcano known as the "Soviet Union and its satellites" shortly before it erupted and ceased to exist. Our part of the world did of course have an earlier existence—the Poles, Serbs, Hungarians, and Czechs, for example, have long histories. But since World War II we had been living in the Soviet sphere of influence, put on ice by the agreements concluded at Yalta by Stalin, Roosevelt, and Churchill, which had left us on the dark side of the balance of power.

The lava began to flow in Poland on June 4, 1989, when the first (almost) free elections were held.

Then the Berlin Wall came down. And the lava really began to flow.

Soon after that, the Soviet Union came apart, and so did the whole post-Yalta order.

We became free. Not just the Poles, Serbs, Hungarians, and Czechs, but also the Estonians, Lithuanians, Ukrainians, Bulgarians, Kirghiz, Tajiks, Kazakhs, and others. A large part of the world gained freedom, for which it was not prepared. In the most extreme cases it wasn't expecting or even wanting it.

The story of the dancing bears was first told to me by Krasimir Krumov, a Bulgarian journalist I met in Warsaw.

For years on end, he said, these bears had been trained to

dance, and had been treated very cruelly. Their owners kept them at home. They taught them to dance by beating them when they were small. They knocked out their teeth, to make sure the bears would never suddenly remember they were stronger than their keepers. They broke the animals' spirits. They got them drunk on alcohol—many of the bears were hooked on strong drink forever after. And then they made them perform tricks for tourists—dancing, imitating various celebrities, and giving massages.

Then, in 2007, when Bulgaria joined the European Union, the keeping of bears was outlawed. An Austrian organization called Four Paws opened a special park in a place called Belitsa, not far from Sofia, and the bears were taken from their keepers and relocated there. Gone was the whip, the brutality, the nose ring that—according to the people from Four Paws—symbolized the bears' captivity. A unique project began: to teach freedom to animals that had never been free. Step by step. Little by little. Cautiously.

The animals were taught how a free bear is supposed to move about. How to hibernate. How to copulate. How to obtain food. The park at Belitsa became an unusual "freedom research lab."

As I listened to Krumov, it occurred to me that I was living in a similar research lab. Ever since the transition from socialism to democracy began in Poland in 1989, our lives have been a kind of freedom research project—a never-ending course in what freedom is, how to make use of it, and what sort of price is paid for it. We have had to learn how free people take care of themselves, of their families, of their futures. How they eat, sleep, make love—because under socialism the state was always poking its nose into its citizens' plates, beds, and private lives.

And, just like the bears of Belitsa, sometimes we cope better with our newfound freedom, sometimes worse. Sometimes it gives us satisfaction, but sometimes it provokes our resistance. Some-times our aggression too.

A few years after I first met Krumov, I went to the Dancing Bears Park in Belitsa. I wanted to know what a freedom lab was like. I learned that:

- the bears are given their freedom gradually, in small doses. It can't be given to them all at once, or they'd choke on it.
- freedom has its limits; for the bears, the limit is an electrified wire fence.
- for those who have never experienced it before, freedom is extremely complicated. It is very difficult for bears to get used to a life in which they have to care for themselves. Sometimes it simply can't be done.

And I learned that for every retired dancing bear, the moment comes when freedom starts to cause it pain. What does it do then? It gets up on its hind legs and starts to dance. It repeats the very thing the park employees are trying their best to get it to unlearn: the behavior of the captive. As if it would prefer its keeper to come back and take responsibility for its life again. "Let him beat me, let him treat me badly, but let him relieve me of this goddamned need to deal with my own life," the bear seems to be saying.

Guys with wacky hair who promise a great deal have been springing up in our part of the world like mushrooms after rain. And people go running after them, like bears after their keepers. Because freedom has brought not just new opportunities and new horizons—it has also brought new challenges. Unemployment, which under socialism they never knew. Homelessness. Capitalism, often in a very wild form. And like the bears, people would sometimes prefer their keepers to come back and relieve them of at least some of the challenges. To take at least some of the weight off their backs.

While I was gathering the material for this book, I thought it was going to be about Central and Eastern Europe, and the difficulties of our emergence from Communism. But in the meantime, guys with wacky hair and a crazed look in their eyes have started to appear in countries that have never experienced Communism. It turns out that fear of a changing world, and longing for someone who will relieve us of some of the responsibility for our own lives, who promise that life will be the same as it was in the past, are not confined to Regime-Change Land. In half the West empty promises are made, wrapped in shiny paper like candy.

And for this candy, people are happy to get up on their hind legs and dance.

Part One

I. Love

1.

Gyorgy Marinov hides his face in his right hand, and with his left taps the ash from his cigarette onto the ground, which in the village of Dryanovets is a deep-brown color that passes here and there into black. We're sitting outside his house, which is coated in gray plaster. Marinov is a little over seventy, but he's not bent double yet, although in Dryanovets, a village in northern Bulgaria inhabited mainly by Gypsies, very few men live to his age.

It's not much better for the women either. There's a death notice pinned to the door frame of Marinov's house with a picture of a woman only a little younger than he is. It's his wife—she died last year.

If you go through that door, passing a cart, a mule, and a heap of junk along the way, you come to a dirt floor. In the middle of the room there's a metal pole stuck into the ground. A female bear called Vela spent almost twenty years tied to it.

"I loved her as if she were my own daughter," says Marinov, as he casts his mind back to those mornings on the Black Sea when he and Vela, dependent on each other, pointed their noses in the direction of the water, had a quick bite of bread, and then set off to work along the road as the asphalt rapidly heated up.

And those memories make him melt, just as the sunshine would melt the asphalt in those days, and he forgets about his cigarette until the lighted tip starts to burn his fingers; then he tosses the butt onto the brown-and-black earth, and he's back in Dryanovets, outside his gray house with the death notice pinned to the door frame.

"As God is my witness, I loved her as if she were human," he says, shaking his head. "I loved her like one of my immediate family. She always had more than enough bread. The best alcohol. Strawberries. Chocolate. Candy bars. I'd have carried her on my back if I only could. So if you say I beat her, or that she had a bad time with me, you're lying."

2.

Vela first appeared at the Marinovs' house at the beginning of the gloomy 1990s, when Communism collapsed, and in its wake the collective farms, known in Bulgaria as TKZS—*trudovo kooperativno zemedelsko stopanstvo*, or "labor cooperative farms"—began to go under. "I was a tractor driver at the TKZS in Dryanovets. I drove a Belarus tractor and I loved my job," says Marinov. "If I could have, I'd have worked at the collective farm to the end of my days. Nice people. The work was tough sometimes, but it was in the open air. We never lacked a thing."

But in 1991 the TKZS began to slow down. The manager called Marinov in and told him that under capitalism a tractor driver must not only drive a tractor but also help with the cows, and the sowing, and the harvest. Marinov had helped people to do other jobs on very many occasions anyway, so he couldn't see any problem. The manager replied that he understood all that, but that even if his tractor drivers were multifunctional, he couldn't keep twelve of them on under capitalism—because until then there had been twelve at the TKZS in Dryanovets. At most, he could keep three. Marinov was made redundant.

"I was given three months' pay in advance—then that was it, good-bye," he recalls, and adds: "If you go out of my house, walk a short way to the right, and stand on the hillock, you'll see what's left of our collective farm. It was a beautiful farm, three hundred cows, a thousand acres, extremely well run! Most of the people working there were Gypsies, because the work was too stinky for Bulgarians. Now it has all fallen through, and instead of working, the Gypsies sit around unemployed. But the milk they sell in the market at Razgrad is German. Clearly it's worth it for the Germans to have big farms but not for the Bulgarians."

In 1991 Marinov had to ask himself the basic question that every redundant worker has to face: "What else am I capable of doing?"

"In my case the answer was simple," he says. "I knew how to train bears to dance."

His father and grandfather were bear keepers, and his brother, Stefan, had kept bears ever since leaving school. "I was the only one in the family who'd gone to work at the collective farm," says Marinov. "I wanted to try another life, because I already knew about bears. Lots of bear keepers got jobs at the farm, as I did. But I grew up around bears. I knew all the songs, all the tricks, all the stories. I use to bottle-feed my father's two bears by hand. When my son was born, he and the bears were kept together. There were plenty of times when I got it wrong—my baby drank from the bear's bottle, and the bear from his. So when they fired me from the collective farm, there was one thing I knew for sure: if I wanted to go on living, I had to find a bear as fast as possible. Without a bear, I wouldn't survive a year.

"How did I find one? Wait, let me light another cigarette and then I'll tell you the whole story."

3.

"I went to the Kormisosh nature reserve to get a bear. It's a well-known hunting ground; apparently Brezhnev forgave our Communists a billion leva* of debt in exchange for taking him hunting there. So I was told by a guy who worked at Kormisosh for forty years, but I don't know if it's true.

"First I had to go to Sofia, to the ministry responsible for the forests, because I had a friend there from school. Thanks to him, I got a voucher for a bear, authorizing me to buy one at Kormisosh, so from Sofia I went straight to the reserve. They knew of me there by hearsay, because my brother, Stefan, had been to them in the past with other bear keepers, and in those days he'd been a real star. He used to perform at a very expensive restaurant on the Black Sea, where the top Communist Party leaders used to go. He was on television several times. Lots of people all over Bulgaria would recognize him.

"Stefan got his bear from a zoo in Sofia. A drunken soldier had broken into the bear enclosure, and the mother happened to have cubs at the time, so she attacked him and killed him on the spot. They had to euthanize her, as they always do if a zoo animal kills someone. Stefan heard about it and went to buy one of the cubs.

---

* When Bulgaria joined the European Union on January 1, 2007, one Bulgarian lev (plural: leva) was worth sixty-seven cents. Thus for part 1, an exchange rate of one US dollar to 1.48 Bulgarian leva applies.

"At the restaurant show, first came some girls who danced on hot coals, and then he was on. He'd start by wrestling with the bear and end with the bear massaging the restaurant manager's back.

"Then a long line of people would form, to have the bear massage them too. My brother earned pretty good money that way. Of course he had to share it with the manager, but there was enough for both of them.

"So I went to Kormisosh. The forester asked me to pass on his greetings to my brother, and then they brought out the little bear. She was a few months old. They're best like that, because they're not too attached to their mothers yet—they can still change keepers without making a fuss. If you take an older bear away from its mother, it can starve itself to death.

"So she's looking at me. And I'm looking at her. I'm thinking, 'Will she come to me or not?' I kneel down, hold out my hand, and call, 'Come here, little one.' She doesn't move, just gazes at me, and her eyes are like two black coals. You'd fall in love with those eyes—I tell you.

"I took a piece of bread out of my pocket, put it in the cage, and waited for her to go inside. Again she looked at me. She hesitated for a moment, but then she went in. 'Now you're mine,' I thought, 'for better or worse.' Because I was fully aware that a bear can live with someone for thirty years. That's half a lifetime!

"I paid thirty-five hundred leva for her, but I didn't regret a single penny. She went straight to my heart at once. That money was my payoff from the collective farm, plus a little more that I'd borrowed. In those days you could buy a Moskvich car for about four thousand.

"But I couldn't afford a Moskvich as well, so I went part of the way home with the cub by bus, which was an immediate pleasure, because all the children were interested in my bear and wanted to pet her. I took it as a good sign. And it showed I'd gotten a really great bear, friendly and lovable. And then I thought, 'Your name will be Valentina. You're a beautiful bear, and that's a beautiful name, just right for you.' And it stuck. Valentina, or Vela for short.

"Then we had to transfer to a train, and Vela traveled in the luggage compartment. The conductor didn't want a ticket for her; he just asked me to let him pet her. Of course I did. But I also insisted on paying for a ticket. That's what I'm like—if you owe something, you have to pay, and that's final. I always used to buy Vela a ticket, like for an adult person, without any discount for petting her. There was just one occasion when the conductor insisted. He said someone in his family was in the hospital, and he regarded the bear as a good sign, as good luck for that person. I could see it mattered to him, so that one time I didn't pay up."

4.

"The biggest problem I had was with my wife. Because I went to Kormisosh without telling her. And when I suddenly appeared at the front door with a bear, she went crazy.

"'Are you out of your mind? What sort of a life are we going to have?' she screamed, and came at me with her fists flying. I gave in to her, and left the house.

"I'd always done my best to live in harmony with my wife, and I can't say I wasn't upset at her for screaming like that, but I did understand her to some extent. The life of a bear keeper isn't easy. Of course, he can earn a living. You see this house? It's still standing thanks to our Valentina. On a good day at the seaside I earned more than I did in a whole month at the collective farm.

"But it's a job that has its price. You have be on the alert the whole time to make sure the bear doesn't go wild and harm you—Vela was with us for twenty years, but you could never drop your guard for an instant. You don't know when your bear's instincts might awaken. A man I know in the next village, Ivan Mitev, had had his bear for fifteen years. He bought her at the circus, so you might think he'd never have any trouble with her— her mother and grandmother had never known freedom, so her instincts should have been well suppressed. Until one day Ivan failed to tie her up properly, and she broke loose, killed three hens, and ate them. How she did it, I don't know. Vela sometimes had hens flapping around her head while she slept, but it never occurred to her to eat them. But it happened with Mitev's bear. Once her instincts had awoken, she started attacking people— the keeper, his wife, and their children. She kept trying to bite them. Suddenly they had a major problem. Unfortunately, a bear has no sense of gratitude and won't remember that you've fed it corn and potatoes for the past fifteen years. If it goes wild, it'll start to bite.

"On top of that, bear keepers aren't exactly welcome among people. We're not respected. I had a problem with this for ages, and I never, ever performed with Vela either here, in Dryanovets, or in the neighboring villages. Only when I reached Shumen, and that's almost forty miles away from us, would I take out my *gadulka*, or fiddle, and start to work.

"So when I brought the little bear cub home, my wife knew perfectly well how it would all end. Women are very wise, and the moment she saw that shaggy little creature she also saw the people who'd laugh at us, the nights we'd spend out in the rain, and us trailing from yard to yard in the hope that someone would toss us a few pennies.

"But I knew my dearly departed wife, as well. And I knew

that if I put up with her outburst of anger, she'd soon come to love the bear like her own child.

"I wasn't mistaken. By the time the first winter came, she was urging me to make Vela a shelter as soon as possible or the animal would freeze. And whenever it rained, she took an umbrella and ran to the tree where Vela was tied up, to make sure the little bear didn't get wet. If she could have, she'd have kept her in the house, the way some city folk keep dogs."

5.

"When I brought the cub here, the worst trouble I had was from a major in the militia—or had it been renamed the police by then? I can't remember—those changes happened so quickly that no one could keep up with them. When he found out I had a bear cub, he came and said, 'Citizen Marinov, I've heard you're keeping a bear at your place. I'll give you seven days to get rid of it.'

"I tried arguing, saying, 'But Mr. Major, what do you mean? I bought it legally. I have a receipt from the Kormisosh park. Anyway, thanks to your economic transformation they've taken away my job, so let me do something else!'

"But the major refused to listen. 'You've got seven days,' he said. 'And that's my last word on the matter, Citizen Marinov.'

"It was suspicious, because there were six other bears in our village at the time, including the one belonging to my brother, Stefan. So why was he picking on me? I don't know. Maybe he'd had enough of the bears. Or maybe he wanted a bribe. I didn't bother to ask. It was all legally aboveboard, so there was no reason for me to give him anything. I went to Shumen, to see the people who represent the Ministry of Culture, and I asked them to call Sofia at my expense, and there they confirmed that I had all the necessary documents. You couldn't keep a bear illegally. A vet had to examine it, and the Ministry of Culture had to confirm that my program would be of high artistic quality. The ministry confirmed that I had all the papers, in Razgrad they issued me an extra bit of paper, and the militia major was told to leave me in peace.

"And he did. All he said was that he'd have his eye on me. I saw him twice more, and then he disappeared.

"All that remained was the training. There are two schools of thought about it.

"There are bear keepers who take the harsh approach. They beat the bear, drag it by the snout, and kick it.

"I was never one of those. In the first place, it's contrary to my character—I'm the mild-mannered type. Second, my father never stopped telling me that God sees all. He gave you the bear, and if you treat it badly, it's as if you'd insulted God. I believe that, because it has happened very often to many different bear keepers. Sooner or later, God will repay you for your evil.

"A bear that's been beaten will be just waiting to have a go at you. I knew a man who used to hit his bear with a firefighting shovel. Whenever it saw the shovel, the bear kept its distance. But the one time the man went near it without the shovel, it bit him, very badly too.

"Another piece of proof is Ivan Mitev, the man whose bear learned to eat hens. He did the stupidest thing imaginable. He panicked. He asked a hunter for help. They let the bear go in the direction of the forest, and then the hunter shot and killed it. And a few months later Ivan himself was dead. His heart. I tell you, God can see what you're doing to your bear, and sooner or later he'll pay you back.

"I would never have hit a bear. And certainly not Vela. My

God! Just the thought of it brings tears to my eyes. I'd sooner have tormented myself than her.

"So in that case, how did I train her? Easy. I just took her a short way out of the village, brought out my *gadulka* and some candy, started to play, and tried to persuade her to stand on her hind legs. When she did, she got a piece of candy.

"She caught on very quickly. Only later, when spring came, did I start to teach her more complicated things. For instance, I'd say: 'Now, Vela, show us how the bride kisses her mother-in-law's hand.' And she'd give all the ladies a beautiful kiss on the hand, which got us very big tips once we were traveling around the country.

"We had a famous gymnast named Maria Gigova, who was very popular, even after her career was over. Sometimes Vela and I would find a place to stand in the middle of a town and I'd say, 'Now, Vela, show us how Gigova won her medals.' And Vela would hop about, folding her paws exquisitely, and to finish she'd make a bow. People laughed, clapped, and took pictures, and we earned a few coins.

"There was also a guy called Yanko Rusev, a weight lifter from Shumen, an Olympic gold medalist and five-time world champion. I'd say, 'Show us, my dear, how Rusev lifted weights.' And she'd squat down, arrange her paws like a weight lifter grabbing hold of the bar, and pant heavily.

"And when our great soccer player Hristo Stoichkov started playing for Barcelona, I'd say, 'Now, Vela, show us how Stoichkov fakes a foul.' And Vela would lie down on the ground, seize hold of a leg, and start howling dreadfully.

"Some bear keepers used to weave in political material. Something about the Communist leader Zhivkov, something about his people, something about other governments. Especially when Zhivkov fell from power, that's when there were hundreds of jokes about him.

"I never liked that. First, better not to fall foul of the authorities, because I hadn't forgotten about the major, who was just waiting to have a go at me. Nobody knew if the new regime would last for long, but the major seemed set to last forever.

"Second, I've always been a staunch Communist. Before the war, a Gypsy was a nobody. It's entirely thanks to the Communists that after the war we were given rights, jobs, and apartments, that our people learned to read and write, and that the Bulgarians started to give us a bit of respect.

"The Bulgarians, too, did better under Communism. On Saint Gregory's Day, the tradition in this country is to kill a lamb. Almost everyone in our village used to have the money to buy one and to eat it on this special day. Nowadays, only a few people in the entire village can afford to do that. At the collective farm, which once employed several dozen people, there are only three workers now. And sometimes they pay them—sometimes they don't. When I hear people saying what a criminal time the Communist era was, it makes me feel bad, because I remember it quite differently. For me, Communism was a wonderful time. I'm sorry I didn't have a bear then. People were in better moods. They were happy. But nowadays there's nothing but frustration. Everyone's chasing his own tail.

"Look, that young man standing outside my house is my grandson Ivan. The brightest of my boys. He's just graduated from high school. He got good grades on his exams, so he'd like to go on to college. If his grandpa still had a bear, he'd get in the car or on the bus, and for as long as he lived he'd keep doing the rounds from Varna to Burgas, just to make the money for that boy's studies. And maybe in a few years we'd have an engineer in the family. There have been cases of the kind among bear keepers.

"But I don't have a bear, so it's a waste of breath—the boy's passed his exams, but instead of going to college he'll have to look around for a job.

"So I've never laughed at the Communists—though one of my friends made fun of Tsar Simeon, who used to be our prime minister. When he took over the government, he promised to improve life for all Bulgarians within a hundred days. And my friend used to take his bear and say, 'Show us, my dear, how Tsar Simeon improved life for the Bulgarians.' And the bear would lie down on the ground, cover its head with its paws, and roar terribly. That was an excellent trick—it showed very well how life has changed in Bulgaria since they got rid of Communism."

6.

"Apart from tricks, people wanted the bear to massage and heal them. If someone was very sick and the doctors couldn't help him anymore, he would come to the bear keeper and have the bear lie down on top of him. People believed the illness would pass into the bear, and that it would be able to cope with it because it was big and strong. And I'll tell you, there was something to it, because when I used to tour the fairs, each year I'd stop by at the very same villages. To this day I can still remember the dates of all the fairs in our province: Rusokastro, May 6. Kamenovo, May 24. Boyadzhik, June 2. And so on.

"And at those fairs I often saw people who the year before had looked as if they were at death's door, but if Vela had lain on top of them, they'd gotten better. They came to say thank you, and brought her candy. And I often used to hear: 'It was your bear that saved my life.'

"Massage is another thing too. Nothing's as good for backache as a bear. The person lies facedown. Then the bear puts its paws on him and moves them from top to bottom. The lady who brought you to see me, the community leader, will probably remember the time I brought Vela to massage her father. She was very small then, and she was so scared something awful was going to happen to her daddy that she cried and cried. We had to pretend I was leaving the house, while her mom took her into the other room, and only then did we do the massage. And it helped. Healing was the only thing I agreed to do in my own village. Performances, never—I was too ashamed. But you can never refuse to heal someone.

"But if Vela was sick, I treated her myself. I knew exactly what was ailing her. I could see when she felt unwell. She and I had a better understanding than I've had with many a human being. I only had to look at her and I knew what she was trying to tell me.

"If she had a toothache, she'd point a paw at her muzzle, and then I'd wet some cotton wool in rakia and put it against the sore spot. I didn't knock her teeth out, you see. The other bear keepers used to laugh at me, saying one day she'd bite me and I'd get what was coming to me. Maybe I really was stupid. Though one time a drunken student tried to burn her with a cigarette. Vela grabbed his hand in her teeth, but she didn't clench them. So perhaps my training was sensible. If she had clenched her teeth, it would have been the end of us. They'd have put her to sleep, I'd have gone to jail, and the student would be going about without a hand.

"I fed her decently, because if she was hungry, she refused to work. She ate eight loaves of bread a day. There's a Bulgarian proverb that says, 'A hungry bear won't dance the *horo*.' The *horo* is our national dance. And I agree with that. You can't expect an animal to work for you if you don't give it anything to eat.

"Once a month we gave her a bath, because she loved to bathe. We'd fetch a tub, Vela would climb into it, and my wife and I would pour in the warm water. She didn't have a bad time with us. You say you read somewhere about keepers who teach their bears to dance on a heated surface. That's nonsense. Maybe they used to do that before the war—I don't know. After the war they certainly didn't anymore. I never let Vela walk on sunbaked asphalt, to make sure she wouldn't hurt her paws."

7.

"I was very lucky to land myself a bear that didn't have to be bullied or beaten to learn tricks. I'd never have been able to do that—I'd sooner have sold her to someone else.

"Luckily, she loved it all anyway. She had the nature of an artiste. She liked it when people clapped, when they laughed and gave us tips. Or when they poured her beer. She liked that best of all. I'm sure at that reserve where they took her she misses those performances of ours.

"But like a real artiste, she did have days when she didn't feel like performing. I'd say, 'Vela, show us how Gigova jumps the vaulting horse.' But she'd growl, whine, and complain. All quite normal—she was just having a bad day and didn't want to work. And I respected that. Sometimes on days like that we used to stand outside the lottery-ticket sales point, and people who'd come to buy a lottery ticket would stroke Vela for good luck. And sometimes we just took the day off.

"The only time I had to hurt her was when I stuck the ring through her nose.

"I drove her to the forest. I lit a small bonfire. I heated a metal bar red-hot. I said, 'This'll hurt you for a while, little one, but it's got to be done. Otherwise you and I won't get along. You'll do me harm, or you'll do it to someone else.'

"There was no alternative. The ring is like a steering wheel for controlling the bear—without it you can't lead her where you want her to go, or she'll break loose, and a bear weighs well over four hundred pounds.

"First I stuck the red-hot bar into her nose. She struggled terribly. She howled. She tried to run away, but I held on to her with all the strength in my knees and elbows.

"I'm not surprised. A bear has a very sensitive nose. What's more, I didn't do it very well, because Vela was my first bear. My brother, Stefan, would definitely have done it better, but I couldn't ask him. It's very important for the keeper who's going to be taking care of the animal to stick in the ring. Why's that? Because the bear's going to remember that moment all its life. You stuck the ring through its nose—that means you're its master. The ring is the steering wheel for the bear, and you've got the keys to the ignition.

"Finally, I managed to make a hole through her nose. It bled for a while, and then there was some pus. She howled, struggled, and looked terrified. I quickly put the wire through the hole and bent it round with pliers. Then a blacksmith tightened it for me, so it would never break. For the next few days, Vela kept grabbing hold of her snout with her paws. After that she forgot about the whole thing and treated the ring like part of her nose."

8.

"Just before she died, my wife told me she couldn't imagine a better life than the one we had with Vela. She reacted very badly when they took the bear away from us in 2006. Neither of us could eat for a month. We pined for her like mad. I still miss her to this day. My wife is in the other world now. She fell sick a few months after they took Vela away to Belitsa.

"One time I said, 'Come on, let's get on the bus and go there. Let's go and see how our Vela's doing. Will she recognize us? Has she gone wild by now, or will she still dance? If she starts to dance at the sight of us, that'll mean she still loves us. Because she loved us just as much as we loved her. I'm sure of it.'

"But my wife just brushed me off. 'I'd have to talk to those bandits who stole her away from us. I don't want to do that,' she said.

"Vela's departure was the greatest tragedy of her life. She believed we'd been done a major injustice. That they'd taken away a member of our family.

"And I think so too."

II. Freedom

1.

For as long as they live, nobody in the Stanev family will ever forget the day when Dr. Amir Khalil took away their bears.

It's June 2007, and on Pelargonium Street in the small village of Getsovo, in northern Bulgaria, the trees are stunningly green. Vehicles have been driving up to a gray cinder-block twin house since early morning. There are journalists, animal rights campaigners, police, local officials, people who have come to stare, neighbors, and also a gang of kids running about among the adults, throwing sticks at the cars and fooling around. Everyone wants to witness the end—as the media will say tomorrow—of the barbaric tradition of dancing bears. In a short while history with a capital *H* will occur, the people who have come to stare will go and tell their neighbors about it, and the journalists will tell a worldwide audience.

In the right half of the twin house lives Dimitar Stanev, a well-built man with a mustache, and his wife, Maryka.

In the left half live his two sons, with their wives and children.

Each of the three couples has its own bear. It's a common custom for bear keepers to live next door to each other and to be blood relatives; they form families of several generations who divide the country into small regions so they won't get in each other's way or steal one another's customers.

Or, rather, that used to be the case, because the Stanevs are the last bear keepers in Bulgaria, and the last in the European Union. Hence all the people who've come to stare, and hence the journalists. Something is irrevocably coming to an end. People like this sort of irrevocable ending.

For his entire sixty-year life, Dimitar has had no other occupation than bear keeping. Bear keepers came to see him from all over Bulgaria, to get him to teach them the tricks of the profession and sometimes to help them buy a bear cub. He's a wily old devil, and everyone says his main concern is for his own interests, but he does have a lot of personal charm. On top of this, he knows the business better than anyone. He's always been able to come up with the answer, and at any given moment he's always known who might have a bear to sell.

His brother, Pencho Stanev, who also has a mustache and a cigarette eternally glued to the corner of his mouth, is legendary too. When the director of one of the zoos demanded too high a price for a bear cub, Pencho went and caught a bear for himself in the forest. Or so at least the story goes among all the former bear keepers from Varna to Ruse. They say it was common practice for their grandfathers and great-grandfathers, but for someone in the twentieth century to go and catch himself a bear in the forest? It simply didn't happen. For years, Gypsies in the Balkans had been buying them from zoo directors or hunters. Catching a bear for yourself was the stuff of legend, so Pencho instantly won the respect of the entire community.

A few weeks earlier, the Stanevs had signed documents at a notary's office to confirm that finally, after a seven-year battle, they would hand their bears over to the Four Paws foundation.

"The Stanevs' animals are the last dancing bears in the civilized world," say the people from Four Paws. And the head of the project, Austrian veterinarian Dr. Amir Khalil, smiles broadly.

The cameramen set themselves up in the best possible positions for taking pictures. It isn't easy: all the action will take place in a narrow passage between the Gypsies' houses and their Bulgarian neighbor's fence. "What sort of shot should I prepare for?" think the cameramen, as they wonder whether to stand on a car roof, have the camera on their shoulder, or maybe get up in a tree.

"It was a real scoop," a Bulgarian journalist who was in Getsovo that day will tell me years later. "You had Gypsies who kidnapped or illegally bought bear cubs. They stuck metal rings through their noses, which they called a *holka*. Bears have extremely sensitive noses. Sticking something like that into their noses is like sticking a rusty nail through a man's penis. And they pulled the bears along by their noses all their lives, as a way of forcing them to dance. It was a sad sight. The animals were obviously suffering. So that day I felt proud that the people from Four Paws had put a stop to it for once and for all."

2.

Everyone has readied themselves to perfection for the handover of the bears.

The police are ready for resistance. The Stanev family has always tried to live in harmony with the authorities. But as the entire district knows, the bears are the most important thing in their lives, and they've done everything they possibly could to avoid having to give them up.

The local authorities are ready for success. It's hard to imagine a better advertisement for the entire region, since the journalists who've come include representatives of Europe's top media.

The onlookers are ready for a spectacle.

If anyone is not ready, it's the bears, who are fidgeting nervously, unable to understand the sudden fuss.

3.

The Stanev family is shut indoors, waiting. There's old Dimitar. There are his two sons, his wife, and a cluster of grandchildren.

And there are the heroes of the day—nineteen-year-old Misho, seventeen-year-old Svetla, and six-year-old Mima. They're sitting indoors with the family, with metal rings in their noses, attached to iron chains.

Misho did some posing for pictures this morning, for which the photojournalists gave him chocolate and Snickers bars. To show how close his family is to the bears, Dimitar's son Veselin Stanev even pushed his baby son's foot into Misho's mouth. The bear gave it a lick. For Veselin this was proof of the animal's extreme affection for his family—a wild bear would have eaten first the baby, then Veselin, and finally the journalists and their cameras. But Misho isn't a wild bear. He is—as Veselin stressed—a member of the Stanev family. Fully and legitimately.

At ten o'clock Dr. Khalil knocks at the Stanevs' door, to transform the bears' lives into a dream out of a tourist brochure—with a pine forest, a pool for bathing, and a view of the Rila Mountains.

What exactly does Dr. Khalil say? Probably the same as usual on these occasions: "Good morning. As agreed by contract, we've come for your bears."

Or, putting it simpler, "You know why we're here."

More important is what Khalil will tell the journalists when the Stanevs load the bears into the cages made ready for them in advance.

He says, "Ladies and gentlemen, on June 14, 2007, the Bulgarian custom of dancing bears came to an end."

4.

In an ideal world, as soon as Dr. Khalil had said these words, his people in the uniform fleeces with the Four Paws logo would have carried Misho, Svetla and Mima out of the Stanevs' house in turn. That would have looked really good in the news, and the radio reporters would have had interesting sound effects, such as the bears' roaring. (As the Four Paws foundation is supported by donations, it needs to ensure that the media has good photos and good audio.) The photojournalists would have taken some fabulous pictures, and the whole business would have been over and done with easily.

But that is not what happened.

First, Veselin Stanev left Dr. Khalil standing at the door and came outside to inform the journalists that anyone who wanted exclusive pictures of the handover of the last dancing bears, taken inside the home of the last bear keepers, would have to pay one thousand euros.

"I told him he was out of his mind," says Vasil Dimitrov from Four Paws. "I said I had no intention of translating that into English. But he insisted, so I told the journalists I felt stupid saying it, but this dumb, grasping Gypsy wanted a thousand euros for pictures. Why dumb? How else would you define that sort of behavior? But you know what? A reporter from one of the

German TV channels just reached into his pocket, took out the money, and handed it to him. Germans never cease to amaze me."

So Dimitrov, the German film crew, and the Stanev family disappeared into the cinder-block house with the cages.

Mima, the youngest bear, let herself be lured into the cage without any trouble. The younger of the Stanev brothers put a piece of bread in the corner of the cage and made a fierce face, so the bear didn't even try to put up resistance.

But with the other two bears it wasn't quite so easy.

"They were crying," says Maryka, Dimitar's wife. "I know it's hard to believe a bear can cry like a person. But I've spent half my life with bears, and I know what I'm saying. They were weeping tears as big as peas."

"I don't know if they were crying," says Vasil Dimitrov, shrugging. "But I do know that the Stanevs didn't make their task any easier. They were the ones crying, shouting, and flinging themselves about—now at us, now at the bears. The granny was tearing her hair out, the granddad kept whacking us with his stick and calling us thieves. Their son told us to fry in hell. I'm sure none of it had a positive effect on the bears. Mima went into the cage. Svetla let herself be persuaded by a sheer miracle. But Misho was stubborn. They battled with him for an hour. Veselin and Dimitar tried to persuade him by putting candy in the cage and whispering in his ear. But Misho wouldn't do it— he stood up on his hind legs, roaring and panting.

"'I can forcibly drag him in there by the nose,' said Veselin. 'But if the ring snaps off, I don't know what will happen. He could make mincemeat of us. Don't forget he's a wild animal. If his instincts awaken, we're dead.'

"They wanted me and the German TV crew to get out of their house. The Germans didn't need telling twice—they'd already managed to film two bears, so why take the risk?

"But I was afraid Misho's resistance was just another Gypsy trick. I didn't believe a word of it, so I said I'd stay through to the end.

"They weren't keen, but they agreed. And once the Germans had gone, Dimitar called his little grandson, who looked about five years old. The child went into the room, said something into the bear's ear, cuddled up to him, gave him a scratch, ruffled his fur, and then went into the cage himself.

"As if hypnotized, Misho went in after him.

"My hair stood on end. I realized that if anything happened to the child—if Misho so much as grazed him—our entire celebration would be shot down in flames.

"All of us—the bears, the Stanevs, and I—were very anxious. I was scared someone would shout, something would bang, or someone would knock at the door and Misho would react out of stress and do something stupid. A bear has two-inch claws. If he used them, there'd be nothing left of the boy's face but pulp. It really wouldn't have taken much.

"You're asking why I agreed to let him get inside the cage at all? But nobody asked for my opinion! He did it before I was aware of what was happening.

"Besides, we were eager to get the bears out of there without injecting any tranquilizers. We were driving them to the park that our foundation had opened at Belitsa, in the Pirin Mountains, for bears rescued from Gypsy captivity. Once there, we'd have to anesthetize them for a while to do some medical tests, and that sort of injection can't be given too often. So as they knew a way to get the bear to go into the cage without an injection, why not? They've lived with these bears, the kid was their son, so maybe they knew what they were doing.

"We closed the cage at one end. Misho was calm. There was just the problem of how to get the child out of there.

"The cages we use to transport the bears have gates that

open at either end. The father told the boy to put his head as close as possible to the other exit. He'd open it quickly, the child would jump out of the cage, and the bear would stay inside it.

"The only catch was that the child had no desire to come out of the cage at all. He was cuddling up to Misho, ruffling his fur, kissing him on the head, and refusing to listen when told he had to leave him.

"The situation was tense. Svetla and Mima started growling. Veselin was in a rage, cursing and fuming, but in an undertone to avoid upsetting the bear unnecessarily. Everyone was waiting for Grandpa Dimitar to do something, utter a single word and cast a spell—on the boy or the bear. Cough, spit—do anything whatsoever to untie the knot.

"But old man Stanev didn't do a thing. He just stared out of the window, looking totally absent."

5.

Nobody could have guessed that this was the very first manifestation of the illness that would soon lay the old man in his grave.

6.

Several very long minutes went by. Finally, the child's father, Veselin Stanev, persuaded him to see reason. Vasil from Four Paws opened the cage door, the boy came rolling out of it, and the other exit was secured.

At last the cameramen had their pictures, and the journalists had their ending—Europe's final tormented bears were off to a life of freedom.

"They're going to their life of freedom in cages," someone remarked, but this subtle piece of spite didn't spoil the atmosphere of triumph and success.

7.

However, the Stanev family did have another go at spoiling the atmosphere. Little Veselina, now aged sixteen, remembers the way her father shouted at Dr. Khalil. When the disoriented bears—disoriented because they didn't know the doctor would be taking them off to the land of a bear's dreams, with pine trees, pool, and freedom—started roaring and trying to get out of the cages, Veselin Stanev shouted, "So who's the one tormenting animals here? Tell me that!"

And then he added: "At our house, they were never in a cage. None of them. Not for a single minute. They lived with us and ate the same things we did."

"But you used to beat them," blurted one of the journalists.

"I sometimes give the kiddies a smack too. Maybe you're going to take my kids away as well!" raged Veselin. "I tell you, with hand on heart, they were no worse off than we were."

Later on the journalists made use of the Gypsy's remark purely as a bit of a joke—he tormented the animals, and now he's making a racket. The tendency among the journalists was to present the bears' new life purely in colorful, or even slightly fantastical, tones and the old one as a stream of endless torment.

"Captives finally at liberty" and "The end of suffering for the Bulgarian bears," wrote the local papers the day after.

Though on hearing that the bears ate the same things as the Stanev family Dr. Khalil could only scowl. His people were happy to explain to those who were interested that it's a very bad thing for bears to have eaten the same things as their owners. A bear's diet should be varied, because by nature they are virtually omnivorous: they eat fruits and vegetables and nuts, but not—as the Stanev family do—bread, potatoes with lard, potato chips, and candy. So the people from Four Paws could only weep at the stupidity of the people who call themselves bear keepers.

The doors of the ambulance specially adapted to transport bears closed. The driver started up the engine and switched on the air-conditioning—set at the ideal temperature for bears—and also a special, slightly dimmed light that, according to animal psychologists, calms them down.

The money for the ambulance was donated by charitable Westerners who cared about the welfare of the Bulgarian bears.

Just an eight-hour journey toward the Rila Mountains, and then the bears' dream, of which they weren't yet aware, would come true.

8.

To reach the Dancing Bears Park in Belitsa, you drive along a beautiful road that winds through a mountain gorge; but thanks to time and water flowing down from the mountains almost all the asphalt has been worn away.

Although Misho, Svetla, and Mima coped reasonably well with the long journey from Getsovo, the last seven miles probably made them feel nauseous. Now and then the van would have jumped on the potholes, and the driver would have cursed the local authorities under his breath for failing, for years on end, to reach an agreement with the regional authorities to have the road repaired.

First, like all newly arriving bears, they were seen by a vet, who performed some essential tests on them under anesthetic: blood, blood pressure, state of dentition, eyes, state of reproductive organs.

They all had problems with their skin and teeth. "One, because living with their owners they ate a lot of candy," says Dimitar Ivanov, who runs the park at Belitsa, by way of explanation. "Two, because the Gypsies have often knocked out their teeth when they were little, to be sure the bear would never bite them. They weren't bothered about the fact that the bear wouldn't be able to chew its food properly and would fall sick as a result. All our bears have problems with their teeth. A dentist regularly comes here from Germany to treat them."

Misho's test results were the worst. "We were expecting this," says Ivanov. "He had almost no fur, and if a bear's fur falls out, it means he has serious health problems. Apart from that, he had high blood pressure and a serious eye infection. We brought in an ophthalmologist from Sofia to save his eyes. It was a success. Now Misho can see normally.

"Another thing we have to deal with is their addiction to candy. And alcohol. Did you know that the Gypsies used to get them drunk on purpose, because then they knew they wouldn't rebel? They did it for hundreds of years. Anyone who's dependent on alcohol hasn't the strength to rebel.

"We had to work on the bears that had been drinking on a daily basis for the past twenty years. If we'd cut off their alcohol from one day to the next, they'd have died. It had to be done gradually. Today, I'm proud to say, all our bears are teetotal."

9.

After coming round from the anesthetic, the bears spent the first few days in a small cave, dug out specially for them by the park's employees. According to Dimitar Ivanov: "They had to get used to new smells, a new place, and new food. We gave them a few days for that before we let them loose."

Before they got their freedom.

For a bear, freedom is such a shock that you can't just let it out of a cage and into the woods. You have to give it a few days to adapt.

Freedom means new challenges.

New sounds.

New smells.

New food.

For them, freedom is one big adventure.

"When we finally let them out into the forest, they never knew what to do, and at first they'd be just about reeling with freedom," adds one of the park employees. "I don't blame them. If someone's only been out on a chain for the past twenty years, that's a normal reaction."

III. Negotiations

1.

Vasil is a touch over forty, with black hair falling onto his face and the charm of a small-town boy who has learned how to talk to people from the big cities. He works at the Dancing Bears Park in Belitsa. He was born here, he went to school here, and this is where he started his career as a DJ, which took him to music clubs in Sofia, Golden Sands, and Burgas. Here at last, some fifteen years ago, he decided to change his life and submitted his résumé to the park's managers.

"At my job interview the man who was then director asked me, 'Why do you want to swap working as a DJ for working with us?' With a deadpan expression I replied that I figured the dancing bears might be in need of a DJ," Vasil tells me. "They laughed. But when they saw that I'd graduated as a veterinarian, I got the job at once. I was pretty bored of being a DJ. I wanted to settle down."

For six years, Vasil was responsible for taking bears away from their owners. He collected more than twenty—almost all of them, including the last ones, Misho, Svetla, and Mima. Only the first two bears were brought to Belitsa without his help.

"The most important thing about the task was always the first conversation," he says, and looks me in the eyes, as if wanting to make sure I understand. Negotiations of this kind are evidently a delicate and complicated matter, and not everyone understands them right away. Luckily, Vasil is quick to explain what *not* to do: "'Good morning. I have a cage here. I've come for your bear,' as I used to say before I knew better. The man might not be at home, and if he is, he'll defend himself. He'll lock the gate. The Gypsy women will start to shout. Neighbors from the entire district will come running.

"In fact, the handover has to be prepared a long way in advance. It just has to look as if it happened spontaneously, for the press and the donors. We took a vehicle, we drove up, and they handed it over to us. In reality, these things take months to negotiate. You have to sit down at the table with them once, twice, a third time, to make friends and gain each other's trust.

"Without mutual trust, none of them would hand over his bear. They'd sooner kill it. There were incidents of the kind. One of the Gypsies from just outside Ruse couldn't cope with his bear, so he killed it. He could have given it to us, but he was afraid—of the local constable, of being fined, of being held in custody. They told each other rumors that we might even take their house away if they didn't hand over the bear. It was nonsense—we never would have acted that way. But they're primitive enough to believe that sort of story.

"So they have to get to know us and like us. And think we're on their side."

Vasil and I are standing on the terrace at the Dancing Bears Park. Ahead of us we can see the Pirin Mountains, with the peak of Vihren rising to over ninety-five hundred feet, and to our right are the Rila Mountains, where the famous monastery on the UNESCO World Heritage list is located.

Below us lie thirty acres that the Austrian organization Four

Paws has changed into bear heaven. Here the animals taken away from Gypsies have a pool, lots of toys, and three nutritious meals a day.

The terrace itself is like a battleship, with its prow pointing into the khaki green of the forest. The greenery is crisscrossed with thin blue threads and dark brown patches.

The brown patches are the bears taken from their Gypsy owners.

The blue threads are electrified barbed wire. Freedom has its limits too.

2.

To get here from the ski resort of Bansko, you have to head in the direction of Velingrad, a town famous for its mineral waters.

You drive under a viaduct carrying a narrow-gauge rail line, which in another country might pass as a big tourist attraction but here just ferries people along a picturesque route through the mountains, between the towns of Dobrinishte and Septemvri.

Just before the viaduct you must look out for a sign showing a big brown bear and the words: "Парк за танцуващи мечки—Dancing Bears Park—10 miles."

Next you drive under the viaduct, passing a small Orthodox church that's locked and bolted, and then a corn field.

For the first two and a half miles you're on a surfaced road that leads to Belitsa. Two towers dominate this little town: one's on top of the Orthodox church, and the other's the minaret of a small mosque located on the banks of the river Belishka. One-third of the population of Belitsa is Muslim. "Mostly the sort of

Muslims who speak nothing but Bulgarian and won't say no to a glass of rakia, but some of them are more traditional," explains Vasil.

The landmark at the town center is the Hotel Belitsa, which has been under renovation for the past three years. "They'll be restoring it for another five," the locals tell me. "Why? Because it's state owned. Nobody cares."

But behind it, at the back of the hotel, stands a line of people who do care about getting some bread and a packet of pasta from social welfare. It's a long line; either you have to come along much earlier or you have to wait for at least three-quarters of an hour. It's mainly Belitsa's Gypsies who are in the line, but there are a few Bulgarians too. I ask Vasil about it.

But he just shrugs. It's nothing new that not everyone in Bulgaria has done well since the fall of Communism. What is there to say?

We go back to our conversation about bears.

3.

"For the first meeting, you invite the Gypsy to a restaurant," says Vasil. "Not too expensive, or it'll have too strong an effect on his imagination and he'll push the sum you're offering to the limits, but also not too cheap, or he'll be offended. There's no denying that they're very sensitive about their honor. You mustn't wound it in any way, or they'll deliberately act out of spite—you'll offer a good price for the bear, five thousand leva, for instance, and he'll say he wants a million. Once he digs in his heels you won't make any progress for a year. You'll need a major campaign to persuade the local community leaders, the Gypsy elders, and their relatives to support you; otherwise you'll never make a deal with the offended Gypsy.

"Better to start off on the right foot.

"Once you've gotten the Gypsy in the restaurant, you must order something to eat and plenty of rakia to wash it all down. You must ask what kind he likes, sit with him, and drink. The fact that you may not like Gypsies is irrelevant—who does like them anyway? Sorry? You do? Have you got friends among them? Well, maybe the Gypsies in Poland are different. Either way, the whole time you must never forget that you're not here for yourself, but your goal is the bear. That's what they taught us at the training sessions in Austria. They even wrote out a formula:

Your goal—the bear.

Your mission—to free the bear.

The bear, of the bear, for the bear, with the bear, about the bear.

"If you keep reminding yourself what you're there for, it's easier to cope. Bears really are wonderful animals, I have to say. They're intelligent, noble, and regal. Nature in its most perfect form.

"So you have to get the Gypsy drunk, which is complicated by the fact that you have to drink with him. If he's going to get drunk, so are you. It's a problem, but for one reason you're in the winning position. You have an imagination; you know where this situation is leading. You know what our beautiful park in Belitsa is like, and you can already imagine the poor bears at liberty. So you can keep your emotions in check. You're not going to start drunkenly hugging the Gypsy in a sentimental way—and if you do, no more so than the situation demands. And the whole time you'll be in control of the conversation.

"If the Gypsy wants to talk about his family, his children, the government, or the price of gas, you'll listen politely, but after a while you'll top up the rakia and say, 'So, when can we come for your bear?'

"As we say in Bulgaria, drop by drop a lake is formed.

"So now and then you have to pour some more rakia. And you mustn't forget the gifts either. Gypsies adore gifts. It doesn't matter what it is. It can be a key ring, a T-shirt, a cap, or a lighter. Anything. It just has to be nicely wrapped—in a large bag, with a design on it, something that rustles. So you keep drinking, and at some point you say, 'I've got a small keepsake for you.' And you take it out. The bag rustles; the colors sparkle. The Gypsy'll be happy as a clam, whatever it is. They're incapable of judging the value of objects. If something's shiny and it rustles, they're happy.

"And there's one other thing that's crucial.

"At some point you must say something like 'I shouldn't really be giving you this, but . . .'

"Or 'My boss mustn't know about this, but . . .'

"And then you fetch something from the car or out of your jacket. Again, it could be a cap, a key ring, or a T-shirt. But from then on the Gypsy will be convinced you're on his side. If you've pulled a fast one together, if you're cheating on your own boss to give him something, it means you're a real friend."

4.

"I had dozens of these conversations with Gypsies. I recovered more than twenty bears, almost all the animals we have at our park. My bosses have total confidence in me. If I bargained for a bear in exchange for ten thousand leva, that was the price they had to pay. And if I agreed to a sum of twenty thousand, then obviously there was no chance of paying less.

"But one time I managed to strike a bargain at two thousand. And the guy who only took that much also delivered the bear to us himself, in his own car.

"What's the most vital thing? The Gypsy has to trust you. He has to be convinced that his own family would do the dirty on him sooner than you would.

"I have to give myself a pat on the back, because for some reason all the Gypsies, absolutely every single one, trusted me. I'd say to them, 'Listen, I've come to you as a friend. I'm going to arrange for you to have some money from Germany. I'll get you a good sum—you might even get as much as three thousand leva. But if you and I can't make a deal, the police will come and confiscate your bear. And you won't get a penny.'

"Then the Gypsy would always say, 'What? Three thousand leva for my Misho, for my Vela, for my Isaura?'—lots of the bears were called Isaura after the slave girl in the Brazilian soap opera—'You must be joking!' Then he'd put on his little act and tell me how young his Misho is, what amazing tricks he can do, how smart Vela is, and how much the tourists love her, how gentle Isaura is, and she drinks beer too. And in his stupid Gypsy way he'd try to extract more money from me. He'd say three thousand leva was a joke, and he wants a million deutsche marks—that's what the first Gypsy I talked to said.

"And then I'd have to bring him down to earth from that million and offer him ten thousand, for instance.

"Some of them would hold on to the bear to the bitter end. Contrary to logic, because the world has actually moved forward, and in the twenty-first century, when we communicate by iPhone and fly into outer space, there's no place for dancing bears.

"But some of them had grown accustomed to this sort of work. That's how they'd shaped their lives, so I wasn't surprised they found it hard to change gear.

"So you say to the guy, 'Give up your bear. Otherwise you'll be in trouble.'

"And he says he will give it up—he seems to have been won over. But then you part ways, he has a chat with his Gypsy pals, and he changes his mind. He hides away at a cousin's place and refuses to give you the bear.

"So you tell him, 'Our country is in the European Union. Tourists from all over the world are protesting against people like you. You have to give up the bear.'

"So he says he will give it up. But next day he says he won't after all, and that just to spite the EU he's getting himself another one too.

"And then he adds something that I find way out of line—he says he knows what's best for the bear. He says his corn and bread are better than our nuts and apples, and that a Gypsy's chain and *gadulka* are better than our thirty acres.

"But what bugs me most is when he says he loves the bear, and that we're trying to take away a member of his family.

"'Man,' I think to myself, 'you're hurting that animal. You're degrading it. You're forcing it to behave in a way that's totally contrary to its nature. You're making a laughing stock out of a proud wild animal! You're making a fool of it!'

"But what would a Gypsy understand even if I said all that to him?

"They'd been hearing for years that they'd have to hand over the bears, and they were used to the idea. But they thought it would just end in talk again. They didn't understand that we weren't going to let them off. We were building a nature reserve. We had the support of important people—politicians, actors, and journalists. And as soon as they sat down at the same table as us—with food, rakia, and gifts—they were in the losing position, because everyone else was on our side, and they were just Gypsies carrying on traditions from a world that no longer exists."

5.

"There's one more thing that's essential. We were very careful to point out to them that the money they were getting was not a payment for the bear. They often sold each other bears, so at first they just treated us like a new customer on the market.

"One of them says, 'My bear is only five years old. You'll have to pay more for him than you pay my neighbor, because his bear is over thirty and won't last much longer.' They'd try all sorts of tricks: if you feed an old bear alcohol, he'll jump about like a young one. So before meeting us they'd give it a bottle of rakia and try to persuade us it was a young one, so we'd have to pay extra for it. Or they'd dye the bear's fur with tinted shampoo.

"But just as it says in every contract, we stressed from the start that we weren't going to pay for the bear.

"'You'll be getting the money because you're poor and we want to support you. You're in a difficult situation. Your source of income has just been discontinued. You won't have anything to live on, and you've got to learn a new trade. Basket weaving, perhaps, or building houses or maybe doing ikebana. Or perhaps you'll open a grocery store or a scrap yard—it's up to you.

"'Considering your difficult situation, we want to support you with such and such a sum of money.'

"We didn't have to do that, because in Bulgaria training bears to dance had already been delegitimized, and we could have just gone to their houses with the police and taken the bears away.

But next day we'd have been taken to court by the organization that protects the rights of Gypsies. And that would have been a fine mess—an animal rights organization being sued by a Roma rights organization. It was better to just give them some cash.

"They'd keep bargaining to the very last. And it's hardly surprising—they're Gypsies; that's their nature. But eventually they'd realize we weren't going to give way, and that the bear was all that really mattered to us, not its age or the color of its fur. They'd notice we were from a slightly different world from them. A world that doesn't treat a bear like a commodity, a world that respects every creature and wants every creature to be happy and free.

"Then they'd finally ease up.

"We had to meet with them once or twice more, for supper and rakia. Just a bit more bargaining. Yet again, we'd have to explain that either they must give up the bear for cash or in a month's time the police would come and they wouldn't get a penny for it. But gradually the situation was drawing to a close."

6.

"After the final supper, we'd make an appointment to meet at the notary's to sign the contracts. But if you think that was the end of the scheming and cheating, you're wrong.

"The first Gypsy to make a deal with us had two bears. His entire four-generation family lived off it; those were the ones who wanted a million marks to begin with.

"We bargained for a decent price—twenty-something thousand leva. We were very pleased, because he was a famous bear keeper, and we thought that if we came to terms with him, it'd be easier with the others. At least a dozen times we told him: 'Don't tell the others how much we're giving you. You're the only one getting that much money, because you're respected and we care about you.' So the Gypsy nodded, drank with us, and we thought it was all under control. He handed over the bears, and he even smiled.

"We took the animals to our park, settled them in, and started talking to the next few Gypsies, but here we ran into a brick wall. None of them was willing to talk to us. And if any of them did, he brought up a price on the order of a million marks.

"We were sure they'd got that million from the old man—he'd obviously told them a load of bullshit. Man, we were so mad about it, but we'd been expecting this sort of scenario.

"Several months went by, and then someone called us at Belitsa to say the old man was at the seaside, near Varna, and—get this—he was with some bears. The very same bears he'd had the year before.

"We went straight there. He greeted us very nicely and pretended to be surprised that there was something wrong.

"'But you gave up your bears to us. You were given money for them,' I told him.

"'Well, yes . . . You wanted two bears. And you got two bears. So, what's the problem?' he said, acting dumb.

"It turned out the old man had bought the bears from his less crafty cousins in the mountains. He had told them exactly what he'd heard from me: that either he'd give them fifteen hundred leva for each bear now, or the police would come and take them away. And he'd given those bears to us for thirty-five thousand each, while hiding his old ones at a neighbor's house in the meantime.

"I almost burst a blood vessel. I wanted to call the police and get those bears off him by force. But my colleagues said that if we did that none of the Gypsies would ever talk to us again. Besides, we couldn't be sure the police would be willing to help. They'd been taking bribes from the bear keepers for years, and then turning a blind eye to their illegal campsites. So we let it go. The old man went about with his bears for another five years before we managed to persuade him to give them up. But we had learned an important lesson. From then on, each Gypsy signed a legal commitment never to get another bear for training. If he broke it, we'd confiscate the bear and he'd have to give back the money.

"Another time, on the day agreed upon at the notary's, we drove up to the house with the police, a vet, and the media, but the Gypsy and his bear weren't there. Instead, there were about forty people waiting for us: women, children, cousins, and some old folks. So we questioned his wife, but she didn't know a thing; she just started to scream and shout. We asked the cousins, but they didn't know anything either. We called the guy's cell—it was off.

"I was really pissed, because these had been tough negotiations, and now the entire team had driven all the way to Ruse for the bear—from Belitsa that's a six-hour drive.

"It was pointless to keep them there, outside the house, so we sent the team back again, while a colleague and I set off to look for him in the neighboring villages.

"On the first two days we had no luck.

"On the third day someone told me he was hiding at his cousins' place, two villages farther on.

"So I went there, but they refused to open the door.

"I said, 'Tell Stanko I'm on my own. Tell him we've got to talk. The police are going to find him any minute.'

"They went to tell him. Fifteen minutes went by; then at last he came out. 'You saw what was happening at my house, huh?' he says. 'When people found out I was giving up my bear, even cousins I'd never met before turned up. They brought tents and pitched them outside my house. You can't give me the money there or they'll take it all off me!'

"I started to think quickly. The ambulance was back in Belitsa now. Another day would go by before it could get here, before we could get everything organized. Meanwhile he might change his mind four times or hide two villages farther away—he could do anything.

"You never know what a Gypsy might have in his head. They really couldn't imagine life without those bears. At all the training sessions I attended our colleagues in Austria kept repeating to us: when you don't know what to do, remember that the most important thing is the bear.

Your goal—the bear.

Your mission—to free the bear.

The bear, of the bear, for the bear, with the bear, about the bear.

"So I asked, 'How did you bring him here?'

"And he showed me an old Zhiguli,* with a trailer, and said: 'In that.'

"I crossed myself, sent my colleague ahead in our vehicle, and said, 'Let's go.'

"To which the Gypsy said he didn't have a driver's license, and if we were caught, there could be trouble.

"'What the fuck?' I thought. 'You've been driving a bear up and down the coast in an old Zhiguli for the past twenty years without a license?'

"But what was I to do? We attached the trailer to the Zhiguli, I got behind the wheel, and we drove off. At first the bear sat there quietly, but later we had to drive along a stretch of the Burgas-to-Sofia highway. And every time a container truck passed us,

---

* Zhiguli is a Russian nickname for the Lada car.

the bear was so terrified that it stood up on its hind legs and started shaking the trailer.

"You can imagine how a Zhiguli behaves on the road when a 440-pound animal starts rocking the trailer. It was swaying left and right. I drove along the hard shoulder, but there were moments when it threw us right over to the left.

"So I said to the Gypsy, 'This is impossible! Think of something!'

"Then he said I should pull up at the next gas station. So I stopped. He bought a bottle of rakia and poured it on the bear's paw, and the bear put the paw in its mouth and licked off the alcohol. It drank the whole bottle, and from then on we drove all the way to Belitsa without any more trouble. When we got there, the bear was immediately sent for medical examination and quarantined. What about the Gypsy? He must have gone back to Ruse in that Zhiguli of his somehow.

"How did he get home? I don't know. I never asked. Frankly, their lives were of no interest to me once they'd given up the bears."

IV. History

1.

"I'll tell you something, but it's a secret," says Maryka, Dimitar's wife, and stares into my eyes, as if trying to read in them whether I can keep a secret or whether I'm going to blab about it to anyone who'll listen. Maryka wonders for a while, eyeing me in an attempt to determine if I'm friend or foe. Finally, she says: "After the war the Communists tried to ban bear training. And they would have, just like in other countries. But they couldn't, for one single reason. My father-in-law had a phone number that could change the decisions of Communist Party headquarters in Sofia itself."

I don't believe it. Maryka must be able to see that, because she asks, "Do you want to know where he got that number from?"

And then she tells me the tale of her father-in-law.

The story begins during the Second World War. Comrade Pencho Kubadinski—a dark, handsome, twenty-something-year-old who, thanks to a year with the partisans, has grown up and become a man—is forced into hiding.

During the Second World War, Bulgaria cooperated closely with Hitler. Its soldiers took part in the Third Reich's invasions of Greece and Yugoslavia. They were dispatched all over the Balkans, to keep order and to combat the local resistance movements.

In Bulgaria itself the resistance movement was weak and divided, and for a long time it didn't pose a major threat to the government troops.

But there were some exceptions, one of which was Kubadinski's unit, August Popov. Most of its members were prewar Communists, who beginning in 1942 regularly nipped at the heels of the Bulgarian troops in the thickly forested areas around Shumen and Razgrad.

In the spring of 1943, the Bulgarian resistance movement, though still weak, becomes troublesome enough for the government in Sofia to launch an offensive. Soldiers travel about the villages looking for partisans and persecuting people accused of helping them. The noose starts to tighten around the necks of Kubadinski and his comrades.

Luckily Comrade Pencho knows a few Gypsies from before the war, when they lived a couple of villages away from his home town of Loznitsa. He asks for their help.

The Gypsies don't refuse.

So begins one of the most colorful tales about the Bulgarian resistance movement. The Gypsies Kubadinski knows make their living as bear keepers. In fact, the government has banned keeping bears for the duration of the war, but nobody has time to implement the ban. The bear keepers are still going from village to village just as before, and in exchange for a performance people are giving them eggs, milk, and sometimes a bit of meat.

Pencho Kubadinski joins them. Whether he spent a few days or a few months with the bear keepers is now a mystery, but a few legends have survived from that time.

One of them tells how one day soldiers surrounded the Gypsy camp where Comrade Pencho was living. The Gypsies quickly disguised him as a woman. They clothed him in a long, flowery dress and a brightly colored headscarf, and so they got him out of danger.

Another says that Comrade Pencho learned how to handle the bears, and they were extremely obedient to him, as if they could sense that here they were dealing with a man of unusual character.

And the last one tells how Comrade Pencho tried for himself to wrestle with a bear, and that he did pretty well at it.

The Gypsy who formed the closest friendship with Comrade Kubadinski was Stanko Stanev, Maryka's father-in-law, father to Dimitar and Pencho. The same Dimitar Stanev who was the last Gypsy to give up his bears to the Four Paws foundation, and the same Pencho Stanev who reputedly caught a wild bear in the forest and managed to train it to dance.

Apparently, they became such good friends that Pencho was named after Comrade Kubadinski.

"My father-in-law saved his life. The Bulgarian soldiers would have shot him on the spot," says Maryka. "He never forgot that. And when the Communists tried to ban bear keeping, Pencho stood up for us. He used to come by our house and drink rakia. My father-in-law could call Kubadinski on any matter. Did he ever call? He didn't have to. Everyone knew he could, and that was enough."

2.

After the war Bulgaria begins to take determined steps along the path to Communism, and Comrade Pencho plays an increasingly important role on this journey. Within the structure of

Communist power, he will reach the very top—he will become one of the dictator Todor Zhivkov's closest collaborators.

Zhivkov's career is like the socialist version of the American dream come true: from poor little shepherd boy to party first secretary. Zhivkov was from a town called Pravets, where he was born into an indigent peasant family. At seventeen, he enlists in the Communist youth movement. During the war, like Kubadinski, he fights with the antifascist partisans, but in the environs of Sofia.

Straight after the war the young partisan becomes chief of Sofia's militia, and at the same time he moves up within the structure of the Communist Party. He is promoted by Vulko Chervenkov himself, first secretary of the Bulgarian Communist Party, a hard-line Stalinist who rules Bulgaria with an iron fist, on the Soviet model. Zhivkov knows that if he wants to go high, he must stay as close as possible to Chervenkov. His mind is filled with thoughts of the top job.

The chance to assume it appears surprisingly quickly, in 1953, along with the death of Stalin. At this point Chervenkov loses influence. To save himself from utter downfall, he proposes his then forty-two-year-old protégé as his successor in the first secretary's chair. He wants to keep the prime minister's portfolio for himself.

At the time, Zhivkov isn't widely known to his comrades, so they all regard Chervenkov's decision as brilliant: the new first secretary will be the old one's puppet. Chervenkov will run the whole show from behind the scenes.

But the comrades underestimate Zhivkov, who has been working on his position in the party for a good few years, and on assembling a group of people who are going to work to support him.

This group includes Pencho Kubadinski.

As early as 1956, on the wave of the thaw after the famous speech in which Khrushchev openly describes the true nature of

Stalinism for the first time, Zhivkov takes the remains of power away from Chervenkov. The speed at which the formerly omnipotent prime minister is deposed by the man who owes him everything is astonishing. From then until 1989, Zhivkov is the supreme ruler of Bulgaria. "He was the longest ruling first secretary in this part of the world," stresses Ilya Hristov, a historian from Sofia.

For all this time, Kubadinski is on his side: at the turn of the 1960s and 1970s, when there are several attempted military coups; when Zhivkov orders the execution of his political enemies; when he sends his political opponents to a camp modeled on the Gulag at a place called Belene; and when he asks Khrushchev to incorporate Bulgaria into the Soviet Union as one of its republics (Khrushchev refused).

"Kubadinski is a highly ambiguous figure," says Hristov. "On the one hand, he probably wouldn't have had anything against incorporating our country into the USSR. He and Zhivkov pushed very hard for the Warsaw Pact to invade Czechoslovakia in 1968, for instance. He was very insulting about the Turks, of whom we have over a million in Bulgaria, and whom the Communists persecuted. On the other hand, he really was a man of the people, and he really did believe in Communism; unlike many apparatchiks, Kubadinski was not just a cynical fraud. Whereas I don't know if Zhivkov really did believe in Communism. I think it more likely that he believed in himself and the only thing he cared about was his own career and his own position."

They were united by their partisan past and their foul tongues.

"Some people are going around saying our power is shaky. A ram's balls are shaky too, but they're not going to fall off!" Zhivkov is supposed to have said at a factory opening.

"Our women have been sending letters to the party in which they complain of having too much work. In my view, if that were the case, they wouldn't have time to write letters," said Kubadinski on Women's Day.

"Zhivkov was in power for all that time because he was good at finding a common language with whoever was in power in Moscow," says Hristov. "It was totally absurd when Mikhail Gorbachev took over in the USSR, and from one day to the next Zhivkov began to preach the need for . . . perestroika, glasnost, and democratization! I suspect that if Communism hadn't collapsed, Zhivkov would have crawled up Gorbachev's ass and continued to run the country."

But the transformations in the Communist bloc had already gone much further. In June 1989, the first free elections were held in Poland. A few months later, the Germans demolished the Berlin Wall, and the Romanians shot Nicolae Ceaușescu and his wife.

Although the entire region was in turmoil, in Bulgaria the only people who openly protested were the Turks, persecuted by the Communists. Not until early November did the newly convened Bulgarian section of the Helsinki Committee organize the first legal demonstration to be held in Sofia. And although barely eight thousand people took part in it, the days of Communist Bulgaria were then numbered.

"Communism collapsed in Bulgaria largely thanks to Kubadinski," says Hristov. "His voice prevailed in 1989 when the reformers under the leadership of Petar Mladenov demanded the removal of Zhivkov from power. When it came to the most crucial vote among the top officials, Pencho voted against Zhivkov. And to his own detriment in the process."

The ram's balls finally fell off on November 10, 1989, officially in view of Zhivkov's "advanced age and exhaustion from overworking."

"In 1990 the authorities and the opposition parties held round-table talks, and straight after that the democratic changes began," says Hristov. But the Bulgarians only remember Kubadinski for two things. First, he was fanatically fond of hunting and honorary chairman of every imaginable field sports organization. Second, he had the first (and for many years the only) off-road vehicle in Bulgaria, a Toyota.

3.

Kubadinski's wartime experiences were the inspiration for the makers of a television series called *Every Kilometer*, the best Bulgarian serial of all time. In one episode, the hero, who is also a Communist partisan, falls into a trap set by Bulgarian soldiers. He receives a secret message from some bear keepers to say help is on its way. A beautiful Gypsy girl distracts the soldiers by dancing while her pal talks to the imprisoned Communist.

"The bear keepers probably did help the Bulgarian resistance in many other situations," says journalist Krasimir Krumov. "They delivered reports and provided information about troop movements, just as they had during the fight for liberation from the Turkish occupation. The bear keepers' songs were a key element— multiverse epics that told stories so gripping that nobody was capable of walking away without hearing them through to the end. They had the same effect as a TV soap opera—you absolutely had to know what would happen next. The songs often had a patriotic tone, telling tales of skirmishes fought by Bulgarian insurgents, of the black-eyed beauties they loved, and of wicked Turks."

Gyorgy Marinov, the bear keeper from Dryanovets, told us the plot of a song he used to sing, as had his father and grandfather before him.

A handsome, rich young man is getting married, and so his family invites all the notables in the district to his wedding. They've invited the priest, and the headman, and almost everyone in the locality, but unfortunately they've forgotten about the Turk, a neighbor known for his nasty character.

The wedding is a great success, a vast amount of rakia is drunk, and everyone admires the beauty of the bride and her husband's riches. But their failure to invite the Turk is like a splinter in the heart of the family. On the one hand, he's an invader and known to be spiteful. But on the other, he's a neighbor, and tradition says that whatever your neighbor may be like, he deserves respect.

The family spends a long time wondering how they should act in this situation. Finally, the bridegroom and his brothers go to see the Turk and offer him various sweetmeats.

They offer him halva—but the Turk refuses.

They press candy on him—but the Turk refuses.

They bring pastry—but the Turk turns his back in disgust.

The bridegroom's family spends several days debating how to act in this situation. Eventually, they go and see the Turk again and offer to organize a special feast, just for him, where he will be the guest of honor, seated right next to the young couple.

Once again the Turk refuses—but adds that he'll only stop being angry if the bride sits on his knees.

For the Bulgarian family, this is a slap in the face. No decent young woman or wife is going to sit on the knees of a strange man, and certainly not on the knees of a Turkish invader. So the young husband goes to see the Turk again and whacks him on the head with an ax. The Turk dies, and the husband has to hide in fear of revenge from other Turks. The message of the song is clear: The Turk is your enemy. Let's not give them too many liberties.

"That sort of song worked in several ways," says Krumov. "It supported the fight against the occupiers. It raised the spirits. And on top of that the bear keepers used to pass on information in their songs, hidden signals for the resistance. Unfortunately, nobody ever wrote it all down properly, so this fascinating world will disappear along with the last bear keepers."

4.

A beautiful young girl lets down her hair and tries in desperation to throw herself into the river, to put an end to her life.

Although she has never lain with any man, although she is a virgin, her growing belly is a clear sign that she's pregnant. In rural Balkan society an unmarried young woman who's with child brings shame and a curse on her family. Suicide seems the best solution.

But something very strange happens. As soon as the girl approaches the water, the river pulls away from her. She takes another step to try to reach it, but it pulls even farther away, until a man emerges from it and says: "Young woman, do not rashly deprive yourself of life! For you have been chosen to give birth to a bear who will work like a man."

The girl goes back to her village, and a few months later she does indeed give birth to a bear.*

This is the legend told for years by bear keepers in the Balkans about the origins of their profession.

---

* From Elena Marushiakova and Veselin Popov, "Bear-Trainers in Bulgaria (Tradition and Contemporary Situation)," in *Ethnologia Bulgarica* 1 (1998).

The history of bear keeping has been researched by Pelin Tünaydın from Sabancı University in Istanbul, who is writing her doctoral thesis on bear keepers. "I remember the dancing bears from my childhood, in Istanbul," she tells me at a café on the Bosporus. "For a child, it was an incredible sight—a wild animal who stands on his hind legs and dances. The Gypsies used to leave them for the night in a small park near Taksim Square, tied to the trees. But one morning they came back to find the bears gone. Overnight the state had introduced a ban on training bears to dance. So the police had come in the night and confiscated them. The keepers had nowhere to take their complaints. They did some swaggering, and some grumbling, and went off home. It must have made a major impression on me, because years later I had no doubt that I wanted to write my doctoral thesis on this very topic."

The oldest evidence of people trying to domesticate bears is—as Tünaydın writes in one of her articles*—a bear's jaw found in what is now France. From the way it's deformed, it's possible to tell that the animal lived in captivity. Scientists have estimated that the skull dates from the sixth millennium BC.

But this was not a dancing bear. Dancing bears came with the Gypsies, from another direction: from India. So claim the experts—first, because they were encountered along the entire route of this journey, and they can still be seen in Pakistan to this day. Bear dancing was banned in India only a few years ago. Second, because the Indian bear keepers trained their animals in exactly the same way as bear keepers in Poland or Bulgaria. They too stuck a metal ring through the bear's nose, just as Gyorgy Marinov did to his Vela.

There were once major centers for training bears to dance in the Balkans, Russia, and Poland. The most famous was in Poland,

---

* Pelin Tünaydın, "Pawing through the History of Bear Dancing in Europe," in *Frühneuzeit-Info* 24 (2013).

the happiest barrack in the bear-keeping camp. Here, at a place called Smorgonie (nowadays Smarhon' in Belarus), the eighteenth-century prince Karol Radziwiłł gave the Gypsies a piece of land on which to build an academy for dancing bears. Anyone who had a bear and wanted it to learn tricks sent the animal off to Smorgonie to be educated. There it would spend several seasons with the best bear keepers, who would teach it to dance and do funny things.

What sort of funny things?

For example, the Gypsy would say, "Now, Bruin, show us how the peasants go off to their serfdom." And the bear would stoop, groan, and grab at its head.

Then the Gypsy would say, "And now, Bruin, show us how the peasants come home from their serfdom." Then the bear would straighten up, be full of energy, and stride along vigorously.

Or the Gypsy would say, "Now, Bruin, show us Kościuszko returning to Poland." And the bear would salute and march like a soldier.

Jerzy Ficowski, the eminent expert on Gypsies, wrote about the Smorgonie academy as follows: "Young bears caught for the purpose in the prince's forests were brought to the academy at Smorgonie, and sometimes there were as many as several dozen animals there at one time. . . . A dozen or more Gypsies were permanently employed in looking after the animals and training them. With royal permission, the Gypsy bear leaders set off into the world with the graduates."*

Elsewhere Ficowski quotes a book called *Images of Domestic Life in Lithuania* by Count Eustachy Tyszkiewicz, an archaeologist and historian whose father "as a true Lithuanian always kept a

---

* More on this topic can be found in Jerzy Ficowski, *The Gypsies in Poland: History and Customs*, translated by Eileen Healey (Warsaw: Interpress Publishers, 1989).

cultivated bear at home by the kitchen." When the pet turned out to have a talent for dancing, he was sent to study at Smorgonie. "Enrolling a student here involved less bother than in Wilno, for there was no demand for either a baptismal certificate, or proof of inoculation against smallpox, and the evidence of his descent was all too obvious," wrote Tyszkiewicz. And he continues: "The Gypsy taught the bear how he should stand on his hind legs. There was a large chamber, which instead of a floor contained a tile stove with a pillar in the middle, to which the student was bound by the hind legs; the stove was fueled until red-hot, the bear's hind paws were wrapped in cloth and slippers, the student was put in there, and as soon as his front paws were scorched, he instinctively stood on the hind ones. At this moment the Gypsy standing in the doorway would sound his horn, and thus the bear would grow accustomed; thereafter at the sound of the horn, thinking that his feet were sure to become heated, he would rise up and perform various contortions."

According to legend, as distinct from the Bulgarian bear keepers, who preferred female bears, the Smorgonie trainers only accepted males. The Bulgarian Gypsies say the females are easier to train—they're less aggressive and don't attack people. But the Polish Gypsies regarded the training of the females as dishonorable. In their view, the females should bear young, so the keepers would never lack bears for their work.

In Bulgaria the bears were not allowed to hibernate, but at Smorgonie they certainly were. From November 1 to the end of February the academy was closed, and several of its rooms were lined with pine needles and branches. There the bears went into hibernation.

The British envoy to Poland during the rule of the Saxon kings (1697–1763) made fun of the state of Polish education, writing in a letter to London that "the best academy [in the country] is at Smorgonie in Lithuania, where bears learn to dance."

The Smorgonie academy was closed down by the tsarist authorities during the November Uprising (1830–31), but to this day Smorgonie has a bear in its coat of arms, approved by the Belarusian president, Lukashenko, and the city authorities are planning to erect a fountain in the downtown area to commemorate the academy.

In the twenty-year interwar period, the term "you student of Smorgonie" was still a genuine insult in Poland.

In Poland, keeping bears was banned before the war, but Karol Parno Gierliński from the Sinti Gypsy group recalls that in the 1950s there were two bear keepers in the camp with which he traveled about Poland. "They did less dancing by then, but more healing," he said. "People in the villages believed that a bear was better than the wisest doctor."

5.

The female bear called Vela had spent fifteen years with the Marinov family—her entire life, because Gyorgy Marinov bought her when she was only a few months old. Each year was the same for her: in the spring and summer she went to village fairs and seaside resorts, where she performed tricks and let herself be stroked so people could win the lottery, be healed, or find a better job. But then Vela spent the fall and winter tied to a wooden stake in the middle of the Marinovs' yard in a state of semihibernation.

Until one day a series of unusual events began in Vela's life, which her bear's brain couldn't possibly follow.

First of all, some people in green clothes arrived, who put her in a cage and took her on a long drive for hours and hours.

Then they moved her out of the cage and into a room where everything was white.

There she felt a sharp jab and fell asleep. When she woke up, something strange had happened to her nose. It felt smaller. There was something missing.

It had also stopped hurting—before then the pain in her nose had been as obvious to her as breathing.

Vela couldn't work it all out in her bear's mind. She spent the next few days holding her snout in her paws. She roared and rubbed against a tree. She chewed her own paw.

She noticed, to her surprise, that she was no longer tied by the nose to a tree or a fence. For the first time in her life, she could move about freely.

She had no idea what it all meant or how to cope with this new situation.

"Our bears had rings through their noses all their lives," says Dimitar Ivanov, manager of the bear park at Belitsa. "It's just as if a part of their body had been amputated. Or a piece of their personality. The piece that made them into slaves."

Most of the rings were taken out in person by Dr. Amir Khalil, head of project development at Four Paws. He was happy to do it. He regarded it as a special moment for each bear—the symbolic restoration of its freedom.

"We always do it under anesthetic. The bears react in various ways to the lack of the ring. Some of them feel strange for several days and keep putting their paws to their faces—they're confused. Vela was like that."

For days on end, Vela kept touching her nose, looking for the ring. Although it had caused her pain throughout her life, she couldn't cope with its removal, as if she'd grown so used to being a slave that she regarded her sudden freedom as a threat and feared it more than the pain.

The same thing happened with Mima, one of the bears taken from the Stanev family.

But there are also bears who feel fine in a few minutes and never wonder where the piece of metal that always caused them pain has gone.

That's what happened with Misho and Svetla. They reacted to the removal of the ring as if losing it were the most ordinary thing in the world. They immediately got on with fighting for their place within the group, and later with love affairs. The lack of the ring never bothered them in the least.

6.

The bears are introduced to freedom in gradual stages.

Once the rings have been removed from their noses, for a day or two they sit in a concrete-floored artificial cave, where they get used to their new situation.

From the cave, they are let loose into a special section of the park, which borders the area where the other bears live but is separated from them by a wire fence. The animal gets used to the smell of the other bears, sees them, and eats its meals close to them but has no physical contact with them. At the moment, the only resident of this section is a bear called Monti, the youngest at the park, who is almost two years old. The employees are afraid the other bears might bully him, so he's going to spend at least another year in the first section.

"It's hard to call it socialization, because in nature bears are loners," says Ivanov. "But it's the time when they have to learn to live with other bears. Accept their smell and their presence. Some of them do it quickly; others take several months. We observe them, and then at one of our daily meetings we decide if it's not the right moment yet, or if the time has come to give it a try."

The first and most important thing the bears have to learn about being free is that they have their limits.

In their case, the limit is an electric fence that stretches around the entire park. It has to be there to stop the bears from escaping into a world where they're not capable of surviving. Within the reserve they can do anything—they can go where they like, eat what they want, they can sleep, they can play, and they can copulate.

As long as they don't touch the fence.

"Luckily, bears are highly intelligent," says Ivanov. "Usually, their first—at most their second—contact with the fence is enough."

V. Instincts

1.

Dimitar Ivanov has a small, raven-black beard and goes about in a leather jacket—it's black too—and he's totally dedicated to his work. When he talks about the bears, he becomes emotional and gesticulates—even his facial expression shows total commitment.

It's not the same when the conversation comes down to the human level. Age? Thirtysomething. Education? Ecologist. Dreams? For the bears to have a better life. And of course other animals too.

Ivanov brushes off most of my questions about human beings with a telling silence.

He became manager of the Dancing Bears Park five years ago. Since then he has spent most of his time with the creatures in his care.

His life's passion is to exercise their instincts.

"There's no other way to return the bears to nature," he says.

2.

"I have a vivid memory of the first time my parents showed me a dancing bear. It was spring, and a Gypsy had come to our small town. I didn't yet know how terribly those people tormented them. I took it as something normal. We watched as the bear stood on its hind legs, the Gypsy played his fiddle, and my dad gave him a few coins. I can't even remember if I liked it. Just that one image: the Gypsy and the bear. That's what used to happen in Bulgaria for years—parents showed their children dancing bears as the most normal thing in the world. Once in a while a Gypsy comes along, with a bear, so we go take a look. What's wrong with that? Nothing. I'm glad I work for an organization that has knocked that mentality out of us. We'd probably never have managed it on our own. It was only pressure from the Four Paws foundation that helped us—they knew how to get a campaign going against bear keeping all over Europe."

Four Paws was founded in 1988 by Austrian ecologists to protest against the conditions in which chickens and animals bred for their fur are kept on farms. Nowadays it has offices in twelve countries. As the first organization to be involved with domestic pets, it set up a group that goes to help them in places where there have been natural disasters—in the aftermath of earthquakes or hurricanes, when hardly anyone thinks about the animals. They also run major international programs; for example, to castrate stray dogs in Sri Lanka, Ukraine, Kosovo, and Bulgaria. The head office has an annual budget of several million euros, all sourced from charitable donations.

The park at Belitsa is one of its flagship projects. On thirty acres, twenty-seven bears live in seven sectors, of which only one animal—Monti, the youngest—was not a dancing bear. He had been kept as an attraction at a restaurant.

"To understand the point of our work you need to know how those bears were prepared for dancing," says Ivanov. "You already know about the rings they had in their noses. But do you know that in the hand in which the Gypsy held the bow for his fiddle he also held a stick, attached to the chain, at the end of which was the bear's nose? The bear would try to keep up with the bow, and it looked as if he were dancing to the rhythm of the music. But in fact it was an attempt to get away from the pain. Their lives were one long, constant pain. And they had a poor diet. They lacked appropriate exercise and suffered from stress."

Now a number of the bears at the park are sick with cancer. Of the original thirty-five, several have already died of it: Kalinka and Milena in 2010, Isaura in 2012, and Mariana and Mitku in 2013. Isaura was the oldest, aged about thirty-five.

They lived with people, and now they're contracting the same illnesses as people.

At the park they are given regular tests to check their blood, blood pressure, urine, and temperature. Supplements are added to their food to build their strength. Their feces are constantly checked for signs of worms.

But even so, situations arise for which the park's employees are not prepared.

Early in 2013, the bear called Mitku began to lose weight at a rapid rate. In a month his weight dropped by almost half. He had no appetite. He trailed about his sector for days on end, looking absent.

The vet began by testing his feces, thinking he might have a form of giardia. But nothing showed up under the microscope.

Mitku was put in a cage, which was loaded into an ambulance that took him to Sofia, where he was given an ultrasound. He turned out to have cancer of the kidneys, liver, and entire digestive tract. He never came back to Belitsa. The tumors were metastatic, and he wasn't fit for treatment. He was euthanized on the spot, and that same day the city crematorium reduced his body to ashes.

Isaura turned out to have such a complicated form of cancer that not even Ivanov can remember its name.

It began with a small spot on her left cheek. At the park they thought it was a pimple that would disappear in a few days. A week later it hadn't gone but had actually started to grow bigger.

The vet tested Isaura's blood. The results were tragic. She was low on erythrocytes (red blood cells), and leukocytes (white blood cells)—low on everything. "Something was gnawing away at her from the inside, but we didn't know what it was," says one of the staff.

In a short space of time the spot had changed into a patch. The patch spread from her cheek to the upper then the lower lip. In less than two weeks it had reached her eye.

Meanwhile Ivanov sent photographs of Isaura's snout to Sofia. "An hour later we knew we had no chance of saving Isaura," he says. "And that we had very little time left, because this vile disease spreads at a monstrous rate."

A month later Isaura was dead.

According to Ivanov: "It's awful to watch an animal that in nature is very strong, and never even has a cold, start to fall sick with diabetes, cancer, cirrhosis of the liver, and cataracts because of contact with human beings. What we do to ourselves, we do to them too. I'm sorry, could you repeat your question? Oh, you're saying that speaks badly for us as a species—you say we're killing ourselves with bad food, stress, and alcohol. Well, perhaps you're right."

3.

The staff at the park say their work involves observation and reacting to problems. But above all their task is to arouse the bears' instincts and restore their nature to them. As Ivanov puts it, they have to destroy the slave bear and awaken the strong, free, independent wild animal that each one of them should be.

The basic problem is that in nature a bear spends three-quarters of its day foraging for food. Meanwhile, at Belitsa the food comes to them ready to eat. But something has to be done with the day.

So a major task for the staff is creative feeding, or, in simpler terms, hiding the food. One of the first instincts that can awaken in a bear is the instinct to hunt. "Well, let's say the instinct to forage," the staff members correct me. "Because they don't hunt. They search for food that we hide for them."

The food is hidden all over the park. In the hollow of a tree, for example. And first the bear has to scent it out, find it, and then climb up to extract it. Or it's buried underground. Under stones. Or else chicken hearts are cut into small pieces and tossed about a large area—then the bears have to work pretty hard to gather and eat them.

The staff also come up with various interesting devices. For example, they fill a pipe with nuts that can only be extracted one by one. The bear has to make quite a mental effort before he gets his fill.

Unfortunately, the staff tell me, bears are highly intelligent. Misho, for instance, soon got bored with extracting the nuts individually, so he whacked the pipe against a tree and ate the entire contents.

"Every minute they spend concentrating is a success for us, because we prefer them to use their heads, not their muscles," say the park staff in these situations. And they've thought up a way to secure the pipe so Misho won't break it next time.

The bears' diet is adapted to the time of year, according to what they'd be eating in each particular season in nature. In the spring they eat the early crop of vegetables. In summer they have lots of summer fruits and other vegetables. In fall they eat plums, apples, pears, and nuts.

In the early days they were given nuts all year long, but they started to gain too much weight. That cannot be allowed. In Germany, at a park similar to the one in Belitsa, there's a bear that's terribly obese—he weighs over 880 pounds. So the bears at Belitsa are only given nuts in the fall, to put on some extra fat for hibernation.

Now their diet is almost perfect, except that it's impossible to wean them off wheat bread. It's a shame, because that's what ruins their digestive system. But they're already so accustomed to this diet that trying to take them off bread might only cause them harm.

Ivanov's dream is to release the real predator's instinct in them. But how can that be done? "Of course, we could release some chickens and see if our bears would go after them," he conjectures. "But that would be contrary to our values, which hold that every creature deserves respect. We'd never do that."

How do you exercise that instinct in these conditions? It's a very good question, to which Ivanov has been seeking the answer for several years. And he has an idea. In the near future he's planning to tie thin ropes between two trees at two different heights, to form a square. He'll attach a dead fish to the ropes. With the help of a special small motor, the fish will move up, left, down, and right around the square. And to satisfy his hunger, the bear will have to catch it.

For bears from Alaska it wouldn't be the slightest problem— they do that sort of thing on a daily basis.

But for the ones at Belitsa it'll be a major challenge. And for many long minutes their attention will be successfully riveted.

However, Ivanov can tell that over the course of this game he'll have to observe the bears closely. "Nobody has tried anything like this before. Nobody has managed to restore nature to animals that have lived with people for whole generations. I do have some concerns. I can't be sure we're not opening Pandora's box. We could be unblocking other things in their minds—who knows where that will take us? Wild bears would find a way to get out of here in two days flat. They wouldn't have the least problem, not even with the electric fence. They have far greater self-confidence and they're more creative. Perhaps one day our bears will go for the electric fence too, destroy it and be off into the forest. That would be a success for us, but on the other hand it would also be our failure. Why? Because our bears wouldn't survive as much as a week at liberty. I'll be happy to tell you about it, but right now it's feeding time. The guys have brought the bread. Come on, you can help us to scatter it."

4.

Misho, Mima, and Svetla, Europe's last dancing bears, spent their first two days at Belitsa exploring the artificial lake, rubbing against trees, and staring at the bears in the neighboring sector.

After a few days it turned out that Misho and Svetla were sweet on each other. Misho started walking around her, roaring, but in a completely different tone from usual. The staff at the park joked that he was singing her serenades.

And that freedom had awoken his basic instincts.

Svetla responded to these amorous advances like a princess who's aware of her true value and knows she deserves all these tributes. At the sight of Misho, she pretended to be occupied with something. Anything at all—eating, extracting nuts from a plastic tube, or ruffling her fur. But she started driving the youngest bear,

Mima, away from the male. When Mima refused to go, she got a few blows across her snout from Svetla's paw. Drawing blood.

According to Ivanov: "We're pleased they're fond of each other. It was the first romance of this kind at the park. What about aggression, you ask? Well, it's part of a bear's nature, and if it appears, it has to be recognized as part of their return to their roots. We want them to be able to express their emotions. If anger appears, aggression is the natural way to offload it. When we let the bears out of the 'zero' sector into the others, we have to expect it. Though of course everything happens under our control—we can't let them try to kill each other.

"The first sector is for peaceful bears.

"The second is for more dominating ones.

"The third sector is for the strongest and most aggressive bears. Here we have Bobi, Charlie, Dana, Natka, and Rada, who is actually a small bear—she only weighs 265 pounds—but she likes to be dominant, and we had problems with her in the other two sectors.

"We sit in our observatory and watch how they behave, and we work it out—how much aggression we can allow them, whether they've already crossed the boundary, or whether we can still give them a while to cool down.

"They have a need to separate within the sector into 'dominating' and 'dominated.' We don't want that, because if none of them feels more aggrieved than the others, there might be a bit of claw waving, and a bit of growling, but that'll be as far as it goes.

"But if one of them were to feel aggrieved, he'd sit there quietly, until finally he'd erupt and attack the others. That has never yet happened here, but it could happen at any moment. Enraged bears are not incapable of killing each other."

VI. Hibernation

1.

There's one thing that's key to restoring the bear's freedom and to all the work with the bears at Belitsa.

It's hibernation.

In other words, the winter sleep into which wild bears fall.

For the staff at the park, it's a major test. If their bears go to sleep, it's a major success. If they don't, it's a failure.

In captivity the bears didn't hibernate at all; they lived just as their owners did. Some sank into a sort of semihibernation, a lethargic state, but there were others that went on moving around all winter, eating as usual, and didn't have enough body fat to allow them to sleep for several months.

Hibernation is also a test of a bear's resourcefulness and sense of his own value. If he feels confident enough to be able to care for himself—in other words, first put on some body fat for harder times, then find a suitable place, dig a cave, line it, and finally fall asleep—it means the work done with him is having an effect.

2.

For bears, hibernation is a natural phenomenon that we cannot fully explain. First, the body temperature of hibernating animals usually falls quite considerably. But not in the case of bears—theirs only falls by two degrees, from ninety-seven to ninety-five degrees Fahrenheit. At any moment, they can easily wake up; their ears are working, they're alert, and if someone comes too near, the bear will get up.

Second, bears do not relieve themselves for the entire time they hibernate. They sleep for three to four months without producing urine or feces. Nobody knows how that's possible.

Third, and finally, they lie in the same position for several months, often without moving an inch. They don't become stiff or suffer from pressure sores. And then they get up as if nothing had happened, and go to look for food.

3.

A bear at Belitsa has too much time, which he has to fill somehow. Formerly, he spent day after day working for the Gypsy. He had to dance and perform various tricks.

But here suddenly he has the whole day to himself.

The bears find this terribly confusing. If they were wild, three-quarters of their day would be taken up with foraging. But here they're fed. What are they to do with the rest of the day?

The fact that the bears of Belitsa are unable to manage time is very plain to see when winter comes. "Hibernation is based on the idea that you have to prepare yourself for tougher times," says Dimitar Ivanov. "You need to build up the fat you'll burn off when the snow falls. If you don't prepare, you might die. In Belitsa they're not going to die, of course, because we'll save them. But we want to do everything as if these bears were living in their natural state. We don't interfere for as long as possible."

Elena, a bear who came from Serbia in 2009, made exemplary progress all year and led the way in her sector as the first to work out how to unearth treats hidden under stones.

Until suddenly, as winter approached, Elena went haywire. When the first snow fell, she started going around in circles, rocking on her feet, and was totally flummoxed. Her organism was trying to suggest a key to this situation, but she couldn't understand the signals at all. She couldn't respond to them, so she reacted with compulsive behavior and started rocking all day long, like a child suffering from separation anxiety. She almost entirely stopped eating, which made no sense at all, because before hibernating was the very moment when she should have been eating the most.

The whole park wondered how they could help her in this situation.

The people from Four Paws tried distracting her, by hiding her food in completely new places. But then she stopped eating entirely.

They tried moving her to another sector, but that just increased her stress.

They tried digging a cave in the ground, to prompt her to do the same, but that didn't help either.

Then somebody thought of building her a shelter—like a dog kennel, but bigger. The staff quickly nailed together some planks and scattered them with leaves. And that was a total success. Elena started clearing aside the snow, stopped rocking, and three days later she went into hibernation.

"Since then we've built five or six of those kennels every winter," the staff tell me. "Last year Seida used one—she had actually dug herself a pit in the ground, but it collapsed. Already in a mildly lethargic state, she moved into one of our shelters and went on sleeping."

4.

In the first two or three years, only a few of the bears hibernated.

Two years ago, as many as eighteen did it.

But best of all was a year ago, when twenty-six out of twenty-seven bears went into their winter sleep.

Of course, it would be better if they knew how to do it all for themselves. "Perhaps they'll learn to do it eventually?" wonders Ivanov. "But you can't just let a bear go and expect it to cope with everything for itself. Freedom is a terribly complicated business. You have to give it to them gradually, in small doses. And the fact that they're hibernating means our bears are making progress on the road to freedom. They're no longer living from one day to the next. They've learned to prepare for tougher times."

VII. Lions to Africa

For several years Four Paws has had no trouble with the dancing bears—they've all been taken away from the Gypsies and resettled in their bears' paradise at Belitsa. That doesn't mean the staff at the park can start looking around for new jobs, because the organization has found another important goal. What is it? Sending lions to Africa.

Dimitar Ivanov has personally already sent two.

"Some people have so much money they don't know what to do with it, so they buy a lion," he says. "The first of these guys we heard about was living near a town called Melnik, and he'd made his fortune selling drugs. Apparently, he used to have a factory producing amphetamines, but once he'd made enough cash, he closed it down and set up a hotel in the north of the country, on a beautiful lake. The lion was kept there as an attraction for the guests.

"As in the case of the bears, we had to define our goal clearly."

Our goal—the lion.

Our mission—to free the lion.

The lion, of the lion, for the lion, with the lion, about the lion.

"First of all, I went to the restaurant to reconnoiter. I have to prepare well for that sort of trip. In Bulgaria I appear in the media quite often, and I never know who might recognize me from the television or the press. So my main rule for these trips is this: act dumber than you really are. Best of all, much dumber.

"So I put on dark glasses and a straw hat, and made myself look like an ignorant tourist, then I went straight to the hotel. I said I wanted to bring my kids there for a stay, and I'd heard they had this very special attraction. And they said indeed, yes, they had.

"The second principle is that once they've swallowed the bait, I let them babble away as much as possible. I just make faces and nod; at most I ask the occasional question, nothing too clever. At this hotel it worked perfectly, because they gave me all the details right there at the reception desk—what sort of a lion it was, how long they'd had it, what they were giving it to eat. Finally, I went to take a few pictures.

"With this documentation, I could go to the police.

"But this is often where the hard part begins. In the Bulgarian provinces the owner of a big hotel knows everyone locally—all the officials, the policemen, and the mayor. So on the day they'll nod their heads and say, yes, keeping a lion on private premises is indeed against the law. But afterward they'll drag it all out and think up endless obstacles. 'Cause, what the heck? Take away their pal's lion? So they'll say the police aren't trained to transport that sort of animal. And to come back in a year, or best of all five years, and in the meantime they'll give them some training. The transformation may be a reality, but some things aren't going to change in Bulgaria for a very long time yet.

"What can you do in this situation? You have to strike a rung lower down. You don't go straight to Sofia but to the regional capital. The local back-scratching won't apply there, and you'll find someone to help. They're also aware that our organization is well connected at the ministry and in parliament, and that we can always strike a rung higher up if we want to.

"The Ministry of the Environment has its local branches. In theory, they're the ones who should be doing the work, but if we were to rely on them, the Gypsies would still be traveling about Bulgaria with bears on chains. Those state officials get a monthly salary of eight hundred leva, and unfortunately their main concern is to make sure they don't lose their jobs.

"So we knew we had to do everything ourselves.

"It took us a few months to gather all the documentation to confiscate the lion. Finally, we've gotten the papers, we've gotten the police who are going to confiscate the lion, we have a vet who'll check his state of health and stamp all the essential documents. So we go to the hotel and say to the owner, 'Good morning, we see you have a lion. According to Bulgarian law, owning a lion is illegal. We've come to confiscate it. Please hand it over.'

"The guy looks at us, then at the police, and then at our papers. He takes his time, probably wondering who to call and whether it'll be of any use. Finally, he works something out in his mind, opens the gate, and says, 'If that's the case, we have no alternative. Come this way.'

"You're thinking that was easy, aren't you? That's what I thought at first too, and I was pleasantly surprised. But it was just that the guy was convinced we had no way of taking the lion, and that he was going to get off lightly. We'd do some talking, we'd teach him a lesson, but the lion would stay there. It was only when he opened the gate and saw the ambulance driving up, with the vet and our staff members, that he finally realized this was for real.

"The guy went ballistic. He started shouting. And people like that have a perfect sense of whom they can shout at and whom they can't. He didn't pick on me or anyone from Four Paws, or on the policemen. He chose the vet. He stood over him as he was trying to anesthetize the lion, and he just yelled and yelled and yelled straight into his ear.

"'Who the fuck gave you a diploma?' he screamed. 'Do you know how to give a lion an injection? Have you ever seen a lion before?'

"The vet was shaking, and I don't blame him in the least. The guy was six foot six, and he looked as if he was about to start hitting us, but the policemen were pretending none of it was happening. They just stood by their car. We were going to take the lion and get the hell out, but they had to go on living there, passing him in the street. And the vet knew that if the guy had picked him as a target, nobody could help him.

"Could I have helped him in some way? Unfortunately not. For me, the most important goal was the lion. I had to get it into the ambulance as safely as possible and dispatch it by plane to South Africa. And that's what happened.

"I had a similar dilemma just over a year later, when we rescued another lion from a private property.

"The guy who kept this one had spent years running the customs service on the border with Turkey. Whether it was smuggling cigarettes, gasoline, or people, he was paid bribes for everything. He'd earned himself a beautiful property.

"We found out from several independent sources that he was keeping a lion there. It was hard for us to get a picture. I circled around it for several months, but nobody was in a position to help me. Until finally the man himself decided to come out to meet us. He felt so sure of himself that he gave an interview to one of the color magazines in which he and his wife showed the readers around their property. The highlight of the feature was a big picture of them with the lion. 'Our purring pal,' said the caption.

"As he'd laid himself wide open, there was nothing to wait for. In a few days we'd organize a team, we'd drive up to the house, the police would present themselves, and we'd show a document authorizing us to confiscate the lion.

"When we arrive, the guy's not at home, but his wife is very nice. 'If it's illegal, then of course, please take the lion away,' she says. In exchange I promise her they'll only pay the minimum fine. She even says thank you. She's about to let us into the house, but first she has to tell her husband about all this.

"So she calls him, and suddenly the whole situation reverses one hundred and eighty degrees. Shortly after, the wife hands the phone to the police chief, and I see him stiffen. And all I can hear him say is, 'Yes. Yes. Yes. Yes.'

"Then the policeman hands the phone back to the wife and tells me that according to the latest information there's no lion in the house. A little later we see a jeep driving away from the back of the property in an unknown direction.

"The owner's wife suddenly disappears, and someone like a head butler appears in the doorway. 'A lion?' he says in surprise. 'What lion? But, gentlemen, surely you know it's illegal to keep a lion . . .'

"Halfheartedly we search the house and grounds. There's even a cage and evidence that the animal was there not long ago— the remains of food, and droppings. But the police have no intention of gathering evidence. 'Presence of lion not confirmed,' they write in their report. We can go back to Belitsa.

"Less than a week later the owner of the lion calls me on my private cell. 'I'll hand it over, but with no police, no witnesses, and no fine.'

"I didn't stop to think twice. The lion was the most important thing. If I didn't rescue it, the guy might shoot it. There were plenty of cases of people keeping a lion while it looked like a sweet little kitty. But as soon as it reached full size, they got hold of a hunter pal, or grabbed a gun themselves, and killed it.

"So we agree to meet in the woods near his home. We drive up in the ambulance, and the guy who's like a sort of butler drives up with the lion in a cage. We take possession of the cage and drive to the police with it. There we report that the lion was running about the town loose—we've managed to catch and cage it in the local park, and here it is.

"Everyone knows what's really happened, but this is Bulgaria. Sometimes things like this don't have to be written down in the records.

"We sign the transcript, the lion gets anesthetized, and two days later it's on the plane to South Africa. And I'm pleased that in addition to saving bears, we can help other animals too."

VIII. Castration

1.

Although the management and staff at the park are achieving ever greater success in their efforts to develop the bears' instincts and restore them to nature, unfortunately it has to be said that the residents of the local town, Belitsa, are not quite mature enough to have a Dancing Bears Park in their neighborhood.

Why do I say that?

Because when park manager Dimitar Ivanov tells them the beautiful story of how the lives of the bears and lions have been saved, the citizens of Belitsa respond with comments that miss the point.

They ask, for example, "How much is an air ticket to South Africa for a lion?"

Or "What's the monthly cost of keeping a bear?"

Or "How much does their food cost?"

There's no acceptable answer to these questions. If the park staff don't reply, the people start to invent sums of several million leva and pass them off as true. But even if they're told the correct sum, things are no better.

For example, the monthly cost of food for one bear is four hundred euros (US$425).

The monthly cost of maintaining the entire park is twenty thousand euros (US$21,000).

These figures are not a secret, but the citizens of Belitsa use them to criticize the park. Whenever there's talk of park finances, they start to compare how many of them could live on the same amount, how much firewood they could buy for the winter, how many pairs of shoes they could buy for their children, and how many free school meals could be supplied—despite some twenty-five years of economic transformation, many children in the Bulgarian provinces still suffer from malnourishment.

When they hear that a bear's food costs four hundred euros (US$425) a month, their hair stands on end. Very few families in Belitsa have that much money, and dozens of them have lots of children.

And when the citizens add up all those large sums, they come to the unpleasant conclusion that far more care is taken of the bears than of them. While the animals are being taught resourcefulness, conflict solving, and hibernation, while pools are being built for them and playgrounds adapted to their needs, the people of Belitsa are being left to fend for themselves. Although they've been learning freedom for longer than the bears, they don't have a team of experts to help them with the transformation.

"I'm sorry I wasn't born a bear," the former mayor of Belitsa, Hasan Ilan, once said bitterly, as he compared the park's budget with the town's.

The staff at the park do their best not to take this sort of comment to heart. They know perfectly well that they're not the people to whom they should be addressed. It's not their fault that Four Paws is successfully raising funds for the bears and other animals, and not for the residents of the Bulgarian provinces who've been cast adrift in the process of transformation. The people of Belitsa should go and complain to their government, and expect it to improve their fate, and forget about the bears.

2.

Despite all these misunderstandings, the staff at the park regard being on good terms with the people of Belitsa and the local area as one of their priorities. They do everything they can to encourage them to visit the park, and they invest in good relations. They put up notices in the town with pictures of the liberated bears. The local council uses the animals to promote the town on the Internet. The park staff have even thought of inviting the children from the schools in Belitsa to come and receive an annual Easter egg.

The first year they made very careful preparations. There were competitions, a clown, a small snack, and puppeteers at the playground. The party was a huge success. So the park staff were very resentful when it turned out that the only response from the parents of the invited children was to ramble on about what would happen if one of the bears escaped and started attacking people and eating them. "Nobody had a good word to say—no one mentioned what a great party it was, how nice it had been or how happy the children were," complains one of the staff. "But they all kept asking: 'Are you sure you're able to control those bears?' We'd reply that, yes, we are—after all, we have a live electric fence and it's very high. But then they ask: 'All right, but what if a bear digs a tunnel?' To which we say: 'We've got cameras. If one of them starts getting up to something, we'll notice at once.' And then one guy asks: 'But what if one of them tries to escape across the tree tops?' Words fail me!"

Luckily, several years went by, none of the bears escaped, and on top of that several people from Belitsa started working at the park. The local people have become accustomed to the retired dancing bears, and it began to look as if relations between them could only get better.

Unfortunately, soon after, the citizens of Belitsa found out that every few months Dr. Marc Sven Loose, a dentist, comes from Germany to see the bears. And once again people began to sound off, saying how could a special dentist be brought in for the bears, when in actual Belitsa 90 percent of the citizens had no money for treatment, and either went about with holes in their teeth or with no teeth at all. "Few people can afford a filling," admits Liliana Samardzhyeva, the local dentist, who receives patients at a small cottage with a red roof. "Usually, they just have their teeth pulled. If someone comes along and I say it'll cost thirty-five leva to fill the tooth and twenty to extract it, the choice is almost always the same—we'll extract it. Though most people can't even afford that. Then what do I do? I do the extraction on credit. Once they have the money, they can come and pay it."

"People shouldn't look at it like that," says Dimitar Ivanov, the park manager. "Nobody knocked their teeth out on purpose. But these bears were deliberately tortured. To begin with, many of them are incapable of chewing anything, and if we don't help them, they'll die of hunger or they'll be seriously sick. It's a really sad sight to see a rescued bear trying his hardest to chew nuts, first with the left then with the right side of his jaw—he obviously wants to, but he can't manage it at all."

3.

But the biggest fuss at the level of "park vs. town" occurred at the very start. The manager at the time was eager for as many of the local people as possible to come and see their new neighbors.

Special vehicles were provided for anyone who was interested to travel to the park and take a look at the bears. But since everything in the park is accessible, the visitors were taken to every part of it—including the observation tower, the small café, the gift shop, and finally the bears' larder.

It happened to be spring, and as the bears' diet is adapted to whatever they would be eating at each season in the wild, there were several boxes of strawberries in the larder. "And that was the trigger," one of the staff tells me. "There were no questions at all about what we actually do or how many bears we'd managed to rescue. Or how important it is for the town of Belitsa, which thanks to us is becoming world famous, as well as for the bears, whom we have saved from barbaric practices. Oh no. There was only one topic of conversation: these bears chow down on strawberries.

"'Our children don't eat strawberries, because we can't afford them,' the people said. 'But they're throwing strawberries to bears by the boxful.'

"Nobody bothered to calculate that if there were five boxes standing there, that only meant a pound of strawberries per bear. Nor did anybody notice that the bears have to eat strawberries, because if we're going to create a semblance of freedom for them, we have to do it through their diet too. When I talk to people, I wonder if they have any understanding of the concept behind our park, the point of the major change we're making here. One guy once asked me: 'Tell me, why is your park called the Dancing Bears Park, when they don't dance at all?' Words fail me when I hear that sort of thing!"

4.

"Officially there are said to be about five hundred wild bears in the mountains surrounding our park," says Ivanov.

"We thought at great length about what effect that could have on the bears in our care—wild bears all around, while they're suspended somewhere in between freedom and captivity. Please come onto the terrace and take a look. Before us lie the Pirin Mountains. Over there, on that slope, last year we saw a female bear with two cubs. On our left we have the Rila range. Over there we've seen a solitary male; we suspect that's his territory. Another male sometimes comes along from the left too.

"It seems natural that if almost thirty bears suddenly appear on their territory, they're bound to be interested. They should react in some way, shouldn't they?

"We wondered what the interaction between them would be like. Would our females attract wild males? Would they form pairs in some way across our fence? Would they try to escape?

"There was something exciting about these considerations. Because of course that could ruin some of the plans we had, but, on the other hand, while we'd never be able to transmit knowledge of life at liberty to them, perhaps the wild bears could do it.

"But it soon turned out that the wild bears don't approach our bears at all. They don't even come near the fence. They take no notice. Maybe it's to do with scent? Maybe the captive bears smell different?

"Perhaps the wild bears can sense that there's nothing here for them, because the females are sterilized, and the males are strange somehow too?

"Or maybe there are just too many people here, and no decent bear is going to come close, even if he can scent a female? A decent bear is wild, strong, self-confident, and independent. Maybe they can sense that ours aren't like that, and that it's not worth continuing the species with them."

5.

"Unfortunately, it's a sad but genuine conclusion—the place where our bears live only provides a semblance of freedom. It's not our choice, because we'd be more than willing to keep them here for a year or two and then release them in the forest to fend for themselves. But any bear that's been a captive for most of its life has no chance of coping with freedom.

"It's pretty much the same for people, don't you think?

"I have no doubt that if one day our electric fence were taken away and the bears were set loose, they wouldn't survive a whole year. Either they'd die of cold, because they'd be incapable of finding a place to hibernate, or they'd be killed by the first male whose territory they entered. Or they'd start looking for food in trash cans and someone would shoot them.

"In Romania, Four Paws has a rescue center for orphaned bear cubs. Hunters shoot the mothers, someone finds the cubs, and they live there for two years before being released into the wild. Unfortunately, the results are poor. Not a single one has survived to the age of five. In nature too, the cubs often die; they can also be killed by older males wanting to get rid of a rival before he grows to full size. And other predators sometimes regard a young bear as a tasty morsel.

"But while in nature from 30 to 40 percent of them perish, every single cub from the park in Romania has died.

"People are a whole other problem. Only a few years ago the sight of a bear in Bulgaria didn't cause any great excitement. It's not unusual—in the Rila Mountains there are a little over five hundred bears, and once in a while someone is bound to see one.

"But ever since we've been westernizing, people have been reacting more and more negatively to contact with nature. A few years ago a guy was killed by a bear. At once there was an up-roar, with people saying there were too many bears and they'd have to be shot. I was incensed. One of the TV channels asked me to comment, so I said that if someone drowns in a river, no-body insists on draining all the rivers. If you live alongside na-ture, you're bound to pay the occasional price for it. And plenty of countries in the West would give a lot to change places with us, because they—the Germans or Austrians, for example—have already destroyed their own nature."

6.

"The German attitude is perfectly illustrated by the situation that arose a few years ago, when the first wild bear to appear there for years was spotted. It had come across from Italy. Hysteria erupted in the media—saying it was wild, any minute now it would start killing cattle, and then people.

"A few days later they shot it, although it wasn't threatening anyone.

"I'm afraid that in a few years it'll be the same here too."

7.

"Going back to our bears: As they're toothless, and suffer from cataracts and emotional problems, they'd have no chance in the wild. Especially as they lack the education that a female bear normally provides for her offspring.

"In the wild, a bear cub spends the first two years of its life with its mother, who teaches it everything. Scientists in Alaska have recorded entire bear lessons, during which the mothers take their cubs to the riverbank and show them how to position their paws in order to catch fish.

"But what could our mother bears teach their offspring? Maybe just that when a truck comes along, there's going to be food. Or that if you can't manage to dig yourself a pit to hibernate in, a hairy-faced human will come along and build you a kennel out of planks.

"Unfortunately, our bears not only have the smell but also the mentality of captives. For twenty or thirty years they were used to having somebody do the thinking for them, providing them with an occupation, telling them what they had to do, what they were going to eat and where to sleep. It wasn't the ideal life for a bear, but it was the only one they knew.

"That's why we decided that we have to sterilize all our bears. It's a pity for us to have to see them getting love struck every spring, and then expecting to have cubs. Then they're surprised and frustrated when the cubs don't appear.

"But unfortunately it had to be done. And perhaps the problems I'm going to tell you about next have their origin right there."

IX. Dancing Bears

1.

The day when his former owner came to Belitsa was extremely stressful for a bear named Dobry.

The Gypsy, whose name nobody at the park can remember, or wants to remember, was starring in a documentary movie about the life of the Bulgarian Roma, which was being made by a western European television company. The director had come up with the brilliant idea that, as he was dealing with a bear keeper whose bear had been taken away from him, they should be brought together again.

"I was present at that scene," says Dimitar Ivanov. "Dobry is blind, because although the doctor removed his cataracts, it turned out the guy used to beat him and had damaged his vision. And suddenly, after several years at Belitsa, Dobry heard his voice."

He froze.

He lay down on the grass.

He covered his snout with his paws as if pleading.

He pricked up his ears.

The Gypsy was shouting at him, waving his arms about and showing off. He wept as he called Dobry "my child," "my little bear," "my darling." But Dobry just went on lying there with his paws on his snout and his ears pricked up, not moving a muscle.

The Gypsy started throwing him apples. Some other bears, who didn't know the man, came up and ate them, but Dobry didn't.

Dobry didn't budge an inch.

"Someone from the film crew asked if after all these years the Gypsy could still force him to dance," says Ivanov. "I said that if they so much as tried, I'd force the lot of them to dance."

They drove away disappointed.

2.

Although Ivanov cares for his animals almost as well as a mother for her children; although the bears in the park have the perfect diet for each season of the year and for their biological needs; although they have pine trees, pools, and thirty acres of park all to themselves; although a professional, ideally trained team looks after them day and night, and tries to help them with every problem, even trying to guess their thoughts; although they have their freedom, and with each day they're better able to take advantage of it—there's one thing the park staff are reluctant to mention, and find it hard to talk about.

I can understand why.

The fact is, despite these excellent conditions; despite the honey, strawberries, nuts, hibernation kennels, hundreds of thousands of dollars invested in the park, public campaigns in Bulgaria and all over the world; despite the personal commitment of Brigitte Bardot, whose foundation covers half the park's expenses; despite the support of other influential animal lovers; despite the food hidden under stones; despite the frequent visits by the German dentist; despite the regular blood, urine, and feces tests; despite having their cataracts treated, and their blood pressure regulated; despite being provided with the correct number of calories; despite the fact that the metal nose rings are rusting in a display case by now, and the former trainers are sick with heart disease, cancer, and cirrhosis of the liver, or are no longer alive; despite all this:

to this day,

almost all the bears still

dance.

When they see a human being, they stand up on their hind legs and start rocking from side to side. As if they were begging, as in the past, for bread, candy, a sip of beer, a caress, or to be free of pain. Pain that nobody has been inflicting on them for years.

3.

It happens in various situations, and—as the park staff say—it's embarrassing.

Sometimes the bears only have to see the shadow of a human being on the horizon.

Sometimes they catch the smell of something, a perfume perhaps, that reminds them of their old life. Who could predict that one of the ladies visiting the park would spray herself with a scent that—let's suppose—the trainer's wife always wore? Or the cologne the trainer wore? Or that one of the visiting children would smell like their kid?

For a human being, these olfactory nuances are imperceptible, but a bear's sense of smell is the most highly developed of its senses. In the wild they can scent things from several miles away. In spring, wild bears are capable of digging a deep pit in the snow because they can smell the carcass of a chamois buried by an avalanche. In the park, it only takes a candy wrapper in someone's pocket to awaken deeply hidden memories.

Maybe they dance because there are too many of them in a small area. A wild bear needs at least twelve square miles to be able to preserve his solitude. Because solitude is a fundamental part of a bear's nature. But here they have to accept that there are several of them in each sector. Most of them have a share that's barely three hundred square yards in size.

It's also possible that the park doesn't meet the bears' needs. It doesn't reproduce their natural state—let's not deceive ourselves, the conditions here are not the same as in the wild, nor the state in which the bears grew up and spent their entire life until now. It's a hybrid, suspended somewhere between freedom and captivity. And maybe that makes the bears feel confused.

Or perhaps they dance when they're hungry or haven't slept enough. Or if the moment has come when their system sends signals to tell them it's time to hibernate, but they don't know how to respond.

In these instances, compulsive behavior, such as walking in circles or being self-destructive, can occur. When Dobry doesn't know what to do with himself, he bites his own paw, drawing blood. He does it when he can't get his head around what's happening.

But most of them stand on their hind legs and do exactly what used to earn them bread, candy, and alcohol throughout their past lives.

Of course, some of their behavior might look like a dance without actually being one. On one occasion a group of school students began to clap and take photos because Mima was standing on her hind legs. The children thought she was dancing, but in fact she was hungry and was trying to see if the truck bringing the food was on its way.

But usually their behavior is so plain to see that it's impossible to sugarcoat reality. If stress appears in the life of a bear, it will try the reaction that's imprinted in the deepest recesses of its mind.

"Will they ever stop?" wonders Dimitar Ivanov. "I think that with each passing year they'll do it more and more rarely. But I can't be certain. As I've already said, we're working on living creatures. So I won't be surprised if one day, under the influence of some sort of external factors, our bears forget what we've taught them, and all start to dance at once."

X. The End

1.

Fall on Pelargonium Street in the village of Getsovo is a cascade of colors that drop from the trees straight onto the house of the former bear keepers. To get here you drive along one of the roads that EU funding hasn't reached and is unlikely to reach in a hurry. In many places the asphalt has been replaced by rocks, stone chippings, and mud.

Although there have been no bears in the village for six years now, when I ask for the bear keepers, even the youngest children know the way. And the ones who were at preschool in those days remember standing by the gate after classes and throwing candy to the bear. Sometimes the bear keeper was in a good mood or noticed a child he knew. Then he'd untie the bear and lead it to the gate to show off a few tricks.

So we find the gray block of the preschool, surrounded by a multicolored swirl of swings and slides.

We find the house opposite, with peeling plaster, a green gate with a vine rambling up it, and a middle-aged Gypsy woman, who as soon as we mention the bears, starts talking in all the languages of this part of the world.

Krasimir Krumov, the Bulgarian journalist accompanying

me, insists that we'll be better off talking in Bulgarian, and he'll translate it all into Polish for me. The Gypsy is agitated.

"They made animals of us," she says, dragging on a cigarette. "My name is Ivelina and I'm the daughter-in-law and wife of bear keepers—Dimitar was my father-in-law and Veselin is my husband. And it grieves me, because it has gone out all over the world that the Stanev family torments bears. But there was no bear keeper to rival my father-in-law anywhere!"

"The bears obeyed him like their own mother," adds an older Gypsy woman. It's Dimitar Stanev's wife, Maryka.

"He loved them, and they loved him," adds Ivelina.

And Dimitar's granddaughter, Veselina, says that her happiest childhood memory is of the spring days when her grandfather would start to prepare the program for the new year with the bear.

"They used to arm-wrestle. Sometimes Misho gave Grandpa the advantage," says Veselina, smiling. "You could see what satisfaction it gave him—Grandpa would think he'd already won, just half an inch and he'd lay him flat, but suddenly, hardly using any strength at all, wham! that bear would lay Grandpa out. He'd be virtually laughing because his trick had worked."

It was Dimitar and his sons who were the last bear keepers in Bulgaria to sell their animals.

It was he who sat staring at the window when his grandson, Veselin's son, was shut in the cage with Misho and refused to come out.

It was his illness that manifested itself for the first time that day.

"Once they'd packed Misho into the cage and taken him away, my husband sat down, clutched at his heart and went on sitting there," says his wife, Maryka. "He went a few hours without saying a word. All the women in the house—including me, our daughter, daughters-in-law, and granddaughters—were crying, but he didn't make a sound. He didn't bat an eyelid. We hid away from him in corners so he wouldn't have to look at our tears, but it was all the same to him. He didn't even notice us."

2.

Dimitar's grave is in the cemetery at the end of the village, among stone crosses dating from God knows what century, the more recent graves of respected and less respected villagers, and clumps of grass that grows on all the graves without exception.

Daughter-in-law Ivelina gets into our car with a clay mug full of coffee and a flower picked by the roadside. She lays it under the picture of her father-in-law, and puts the mug down on the small gravestone.

"Whenever he saw me, he'd say, 'Dearest daughter-in-law, make me some coffee!'" she tells us. "Sometimes three or four times a day. So every time I come here, I bring him coffee. The way he liked it—one and a half spoonfuls, with no milk and no sugar."

"We put an accordion in the coffin for him, because he'd played it beautifully since childhood," says his wife, wiping her eyes. "I'm sorry, normally I don't cry at his grave anymore. But today there are the memories of Saint Dimitar's Day. We always had a jolly time on this day—we drank and sang. Our bears had something good to eat too. They'd dance for us. We were happy. But nowadays? The bears are gone, so is my husband, and so are our children. Our sons have had to go away to Greece because there are no job prospects here at all. Most of the former bear keepers have left. Pencho, my husband's brother, drove a tanker truck to begin with, but now he's in Greece, working on a building site. Stefan, our brother-in-law, is in Italy. He was working at a gas station, but now he's sick."

I look at the picture of Dimitar. Stuck to the terrazzo head-stone is a photograph of a well-built man with a mustache, stand-ing next to Misho, on his hind paws, feet apart. The caption says: "For Dimitar, who entertained the children for many years from Varna to Golden Sands with his dancing bear."

In one hand Dimitar is holding a chain that's tied to Misho's nose.

In the other, he has the fiddle he always played to accom-pany the bear's dance.

"Oh yes, a fiddle! What happened to Dimitar's *gadulka*?" I ask, and Krasimir translates my question for the Gypsies.

"He took the accordion with him. I'll be bringing him the *gadulka*," says Maryka.

From this point on, the whole way back to their house, none of us says a word.

3.

Dimitar Stanev began to fall ill as soon as the bears left.

"And he had always been the healthiest in the family," says Maryka. "He could sleep outside until late into the fall, covered with any old thing, and never so much as caught a cold. His star turn was wrestling with a bear. The only man who could arm-wrestle everyone in the district, but suddenly he was as weak as a blade of grass."

He went to Razgrad to see a doctor. Then to Shumen, then Varna.

He wandered about the house as if he wasn't there. He'd start talking, then forget in mid-sentence what he wanted to say.

"Grandpa always played the accordion beautifully," says his

granddaughter. "One spring, about two years after they took the bears away from us, he finally got up in a good mood. He said you have to go on living. He put on his folk costume, picked up his concertina, and first he went to Varna, then he called to say he was going to Greece with some friends. There he went about the restaurants with his accordion, singing and collecting money."

"He was gone for six weeks," says his wife. "He came back even sadder. 'I felt like a fool,' he said. 'Those songs can't be sung without a bear.'"

And he sank into himself again.

In a year he amassed a whole bag full of medicines. One for high blood pressure, another for liver function, a third for the kidneys. The family still keeps the bag—the kind made of imitation leather. They haven't the strength to throw it away.

Perhaps if Dimitar had lived in another country, he'd have found a doctor who'd have diagnosed him with depression, prescribed drugs that would have improved his mood, and maybe even a few therapy sessions, at which he could have talked about his pain after the bears left. Perhaps a therapist could have helped him to deal with the trauma, just as they help the relatives of people who are killed in car accidents or who die of cancer. After all, Misho was part of his life for nineteen years.

Perhaps if the organization that took away the bears worked in a slightly different way, they'd have suggested that sort of help for him. It's not hard to guess that if someone has practiced a single profession all his life, it's hard for him to come up with anything new overnight. Even if we regard his work as barbaric, it's impossible to deny that Dimitar had a profound relationship with Misho.

But Four Paws only thinks about the animals. When asked about the bear keepers, they say there are special organizations that take care of Roma rights. The bear keepers should apply to them.

4.

A few months after coming back from Greece, Dimitar had his first heart attack. He keeled over in the kitchen, between the table and the fridge.

He was taken to Razgrad by ambulance. The doctors said his heart was falling apart and that next time he had a heart attack—which was only a matter of time—he wouldn't survive.

Dimitar went home, with even more drugs and orders not to get upset about anything. He stopped watching the news. He stopped listening to the radio. He even tried not to drink coffee.

It was a minor stroke that landed him in a hospital in Varna. He never came home again.

"Grandpa died last year, of longing. Longing for Misho," says Veselina, faltering with emotion. And crying.

Misho is not capable of getting his head around Dimitar's death. Probably all he knows is that the man was there, for a long time, sometimes as a jab in the side, sometimes as a piece of candy, sometimes as a slice of bread, and then suddenly that man was gone.

Sometimes the man comes back to him, in a smell or in a flavor. Then Misho loses his reason for a while. But that doesn't stop him from making excellent progress on the road to freedom.

He has a proper bear's diet. He has learned to hibernate and can even dig himself a den. The roots of his teeth, which prevented him from chewing tougher bits of meat, have been extracted by a professional dentist, and the hole made by the nose ring has healed up.

When spring comes, Misho wakes from his lethargy and goes to find Svetla. He circles her like a shy teenager. Now he goes closer, now he moves away again. He roars, rubs against a tree, and goes up to her again. Svetla patiently watches the performance.

Until they come together.

Their attempt to continue the species doesn't last long. Once it's over, Svetla plunges into a state of bliss for several weeks. Only after a month or two does she realize something hasn't gone right. Then both she and Misho start to dance, each in a different corner of the park for dancing bears at Belitsa, the park that's like something out of a tourist brochure.

Part Two

Part Two

I. Love

She always had more than enough bread. The best
alcohol. Strawberries. Chocolate. Candy bars. I'd
have carried her on my back if I only could. So if
you say I beat her, or that she had a bad time with
me, you're lying.

Cuba: The McRevolution Is Coming

"El Barbudo"—the bearded one—"won't drag on for much longer," people are saying all the way from Guantánamo to Pinar del Río.

"He's dead already, they're just afraid to say. So the nation won't go crazy with grief," quips Alfonso, a cab driver from Havana. He's sure of Fidel's death: a friend's brother-in-law is a paramedic at the government hospital, and apparently he saw Fidel with his own eyes. According to the brother-in-law, Castro was dying. "High up the ladder they're already discussing who will replace him and what sort of new regime we'll have," says Alfonso. "Because the fact that Communism has failed is obvious. But they can't just introduce capitalism here overnight either—that would be as if someone who hasn't eaten for ages were suddenly given five hamburgers all at once. The stomach can't cope with it. In short, our politicians have to prepare for these changes."

"How are they to do that?"

"Well, the way it's always done in similar situations. Making sure they'll retain some privileges. That no one will take away their fortunes. That their people will be able to found businesses. If they can work it out, we'll have changes here. Like in Poland, like in Germany, like in Romania."

"Which politicians? Raúl Castro?"

"Nooo," says Alfonso, pouting. "It's already happening behind his back. The Castro brothers are mentally stuck at the level of the Cold War. The guys who are working it all out between them are the sort of people whose names neither you nor I are aware of. I know a guy who has a decent car, and he sometimes drives them. Jackals. Well dressed, plenty of cash. That's how it always works—you ought to know." And Alfonso casts me a reproachful glance, as if he's looking at someone who's clueless about life. That's probably how I appear in his eyes: not only, despite the assurances of the brother-in-law, do I not believe in Castro's death, but I don't even know how regimes change.

Maria, who owns a small stall selling eggs in downtown Havana is of a different opinion. "Fidel is alive," she says. "But he can't understand what's going on around him. He's being kept alive artificially. And, it's true, by now the decisions are made behind his back."

Maria claims to know the driver who took Castro to the hospital. "They put a pen in his hand to make him sign things, but it's Raúl moving the hand," she says with unwavering certainty.

"All that's nonsense," fumes Mirurgia, a true Communist. Her husband works at one of the ministries, and so—as she claims—he has access to the latest, most definite information. "Fidel Castro is getting better and better, and all his enemies will be surprised how much good he's still going to do for Cuba. He'll live to a hundred and ten or maybe more. Nobody's going to crush our revolution," she says, her dewlap all but quivering with indignation that anyone could think differently.

There are just as many opinions as there are people. Just as many more or less imaginary friends, each of whom has access to information from the summit of power. And just as many ideas about what will happen to Cuba when the older Castro brother finally dies.

Brushes instead of indicators

In the tourist town of Varadero I rented a car, the cheapest on offer—a Peugeot 206.

Although it was cheap, its red registration plates made me into a superman.

First of all, renting a car for ten days costs the same amount as a traffic cop earns in two years. Second, it's mainly tourists who drive around Cuba with red registration plates, and a good many Cubans make their living from tourists. That's probably why I was only stopped once by a policeman. I brazenly ran into him while driving the wrong way. He saluted and politely asked me not to do it again. He seemed fearful.

Third, a car in Cuba is a rarity. The buses run infrequently, and irregularly, and they often break down. When they run out of lightbulbs for their indicators, the drivers fix brushes to a string and then pull it, from the left or the right, if they want to make a turn. And that's if they know where to buy the brush. Anyone who has to go anywhere hitches a ride. There are even special shelters for hitchhikers, so-called alternative transport points. A uniformed employee stops the cars and assigns seats.

You wait for hours. That's why anyone who could squeezed into my car. In eight days my passengers included

> twenty-five farmworkers;
> six policemen in uniform and one in plain clothes;
> four engineers;
> eight nurses and two doctors—all in white tunics;
> one priest, assistant to the local bishop;
> six soldiers;
> twelve kids, on their way to or from school;
> three pregnant women and four carrying babies;
> twelve retired people, and many others.

> In total, well over one hundred people.

The true Communist: may Fidel live for as long as possible!

I'm on the road from Santiago de Cuba to the Sierra Maestra, where Fidel conducted his revolution. From here, in 1959, he set off to conquer Havana, and he and his guerrillas launched the ultimate storm against the American-backed troops of President Fulgencio Batista.

The jungle here is virginally audacious and unrestrained, making me feel that if I were to stop the car for half an hour, it would force its way inside, destroy the upholstery, and open its jaws wide enough to scarf me down, Peugeot and all. Everything here is intensely green—there's not just one but dozens of different shades of green, with brightly colored birds moving around in it, like commas in a sentence.

It's a place created to remain wild. The road seems absurd

here, a gray-and-blue ribbon that someone has accidentally dropped among mountains coated with foliage and flecked with multicolored birds. Standing by this road I see a stout, stylish, black woman of over fifty. I stop and invite her to get in. She carefully settles herself, adjusts her suit and the pillbox hat that's pinned to her raven-black hair, and we drive off in the direction of the nearest small town.

"Witek," I introduce myself by my nickname, once my guest is sitting comfortably. I already know that her name is Mirurgia, and she's on her way home from visiting her mother, who lives in these mountains.

"Fidek?" she says, unable to pronounce my name.

"No, not Fidel. But while we're on the subject of El Comandante . . . ," I say, smiling to myself.

This is how I start a conversation about the dying Castro. A direct question would be inappropriate—criticism of El Barbudo carries the risk of jail. But, perhaps emotionally stirred by the illness, and what looks like the imminent demise of the older Castro brother, people are talking to me in a surprisingly frank and open way. Both those who love Castro and those who wish him ill.

Mirurgia belongs to the former category.

"I wish he had twice as long a life ahead of him," she says with a tone of regret, and adjusts her hat again.

"Why is that?"

"Thanks to him, we're the last country that isn't led on a string by the USA. We have a superb education and health-care system. Nobody's dying of hunger here. You only have to look at Dominica, or Haiti, which are on America's leash. They've got nothing to eat there. But in the stores here you can buy anything . . ."

Mirurgia is the most genuine Communist I've ever met.

She's a party member, head of her local Committee for the Defense of the Revolution, and wife of a civil servant working at a ministry. A badge with a revolutionary star pinned to the lapel of her suit adds to her dignity. She even has a picture of Fidel in her wallet. She shows it to me: Fidel, still young, with a cigar, his beard flecked with gray.

"Yes, but ordinary Cubans don't have access to those stores," I tell her. "You can only get everything in tourist stores, for *pesos convertibles*," hard currency for foreigners. "I've seen empty shelves in the stores that are for everyone."

"Of course, we do have some problems. The Americans do everything they can to weaken our economy . . ."

"What does your economy rely on?"

"Sugarcane, tobacco, the best cigars in the world. Is that enough?"

"To feed eleven million people? Well, I don't know . . ."

"There are the tourists too. Well over two million. They travel around the entire coast; in Havana they're in every other restaurant. Even here, in the Sierra Maestra, my mother sees them almost every day."

It's true. Fidel started letting them in after the collapse of the USSR, when Cuba was on the brink of destitution. Foreigners began to appear at the abandoned resorts again, and the wallets of those in power started to fill with cash. For Raúl Castro's people, mainly from the military, are the ones behind the tourist boom.

"If life's so good, why are there so many beggars here? Why are there so many *jineteras*—prostitutes?"

"Because they have no honor," says Mirurgia indignantly. "They want to be given money for nothing, but in Cuba you have to work. An honest person earns a living by working, not—forgive me—by selling their ass. My parents lived in the countryside, and there was terrible poverty. There were times when we ate soup made of tree bark. Everything I have today I gained through hard work. I finished school, and I went to college. I'm a construction engineer, I build houses, and my greatest pride is the city hospital in Havana. I was responsible for a whole floor of it, and Fidel himself congratulated me. Is that possible in any other country in the Caribbean? In those places they're still eating bark to this day. But may our *palomito* live for two hundred years! Without him they'll turn this country into a bordello."

The host: time costs money

As I was having my breakfast in Matanzas, a tourist paradise located on a bay of the same name, a provocatively dressed young woman arrived at the guesthouse. She looked about seventeen. She'd been lured in by the car with red registration plates. She started telling me about her grandmother who was seriously sick, and to whom I absolutely had to drive her. I wanted to help and was already putting on my shoes, when my host stopped me.

"She'd have made you drive around the district until something happened between you," he explained later. "Whether it happened or not, you'd have had to give her some money. For the time spent together. Lots of people try to earn money like that around here."

The precedent for extracting money from foreigners comes from above. For years on end, Fidel lived on Soviet rubles. When the Soviet Union collapsed, he found a new sponsor, Hugo Chávez of Venezuela. Fidel's German biographer, Volker Skierka, cites this anecdote: "The name of the Cuban citizen Fidel Castro first entered the White House files in 1940. On November 6 of that year the young boarder at the Jesuit Dolores College in Santiago de Cuba sent a three-page letter to US President Franklin D. Roosevelt congratulating him on his re-election. Before signing off, with a bold flourish, 'Goodby Your friend,' he added a personal request: 'If you like, give me a ten dollars bill American . . . I would like to have one of them.' . . . He received no reply from the president, only a letter of thanks from the State Department. Nor did it contain a ten-dollar bill. No one could then suspect that the boy would grow up and confiscate everything that the North Americans owned in Cuba."*

"He also confiscated everything that the Cubans owned. So they 'confiscate' whatever they can from the tourists. It's a sort of historical justice," laughs the rep for one of the tourist companies.

The worker: I'd exchange my wife

José Mendoza, a handsome man of mixed race, is sprawling on the backseat like the king of low-capacity cars. He got into my Peugeot at the side of the major highway from Matanzas to Santa Clara, known as the Autopista Nacional. Outside the windows of our little car, as it blazes along at sixty miles per hour, the shadows of palm trees, extremely long at this time of day, flash by. We pass several immense sugarcane plantations, to which the workers are driven in big Soviet ZIL trucks. At the sight of his pals, José shouts loudly, waves his arms, and swells with pride that today he's not traveling with them but with me.

"It's the first time I've been in a car that has a machine to

---

* Volker Skierka, *Fidel Castro: A Biography*, translated by Patrick Camiller (Cambridge: Polity, 2006).

Bear keepers on the way to work . . .

. . . and at home before leaving.

Stefan Marinov wrestling with a bear . . .

. . . and after winning the fight.

Stefan bought his bear from a zoo in Sofia when she was only a few months old. The bear's mother was euthanized when she killed a drunken soldier who broke into her enclosure.

Gyorgy Marinov with his beloved Vela.

A bear working at one of the Bulgarian resorts.

Pencho Stanev with the female bear that he apparently took straight from the forest when the zoo wanted too much money for a cub.

A moment of relaxation in the lap of nature.

Pencho with tourists on the Black Sea.

make it cold inside," he says, smiling, as he feels the breeze from the air-conditioning on his skin. "I usually go to work squeezed in like a sardine. I work at the Fernando de Dios Agro-Industrial Complex, a big sugarcane plantation. Every morning a ZIL goes round the villages picking us up, and if it doesn't break down, it gets us to work by eight."

"Is it good work?"

"It's tough. We cut the cane with machetes. I spend ten hours a day waving a machete, with a short break at the hottest time."

"How much do you earn?"

"Ten dollars. A month."

"Is that enough?"

"My wife works too. And I earn extra money as a bricklayer. When there's no harvest, I can double or even triple my salary. Thirty dollars is plenty, isn't it? Everyone has to do extra work here. My brother sells cheese by the highway. My brother-in-law sells gasoline on the side from his company truck. My aunt rears chickens and takes them to the market at Holguín. My wife writes official letters for people, and my father-in-law cuts people's hair."

"Is there anything you'd change about your life?"

"I'd exchange my wife—I'm bored with her. And my job. I'd rather do more bricklaying and less work with the sugarcane. But I can't complain. My life's pretty much okay. I can't complain about the plantation. I met my wife, and my girlfriend, there. First my wife. She's our bookkeeper. And recently I met Juana, a *machetera* from the women's group. We produced a wall newspaper together for Fidel's birthday. We went to Holguín together to fetch a comrade from Havana who came to give a talk on the significance of sugarcane production for the continuity of the revolution. Today, for the first time, we're meeting in Holguín for a date."

"And what do you think about Fidel's health?"

"May he live to be one hundred and fifty!" says José enthusiastically. But soon after, he clams up.

"What's up with you?" I ask.

"Oh, nothing . . . You know, sometimes it's hard for me to make the break from home to the city. And I was just thinking,"—at this point he smiles mischievously—"when Fidel dies, we're sure to have to do another wall newspaper."

The salsa queen: my fingernails for Fidel

Bracelets, beads, shells, and scarves; artificial curls mixed with natural ones; huge earrings and great long fingernails. Ana, top salsa dancer and teacher, the most colorful person I've ever seen in my life, sits stiffly with her legs straight and her arm slightly bent to one side. Beside her sits her husband and partner, Oswaldo.

Two hours ago they were standing by the road, cursing. They were on their way home from Varadero, where they'd been dancing at one of the hotels. In exchange for a lift they've invited me in for a mojito and a salsa demonstration.

The boom box roars away as the room fills with sound. First come the drums, then the trumpets join in, and soon after Ibrahim Ferrer from the Buena Vista Social Club (whom my hosts apparently knew in person) sings about a love that's tough but worth the sacrifice. Oswaldo takes a step forward, Ana retreats and shakes her head to say no. Disconcerted, he takes a step back. Then she goes forward. And so on, over and over, several times, to depict the fight between the lovers, whose problem is that they both want to make the first move. The music picks up speed, and so do the dancers. Finally, they embrace tightly as they reach the finale and the bravos. The guests applaud, including their son and his girlfriend, their daughter and her children, and several tourists.

The demonstration was for potential clients of Ana's Salsa School. A lesson costs ten pesos (fifty cents) per hour. All in a tiny room, which by day is the salsa academy and at night becomes their apartment. There's a kettle, a phone, and an old fridge. On the walls and closets there are traditional Cuban dolls dressed like girls at a carnival.

"I have music in my genes," says Ana. "Before the war my grandfather was a famous jazz player and showman. His star turn was playing the drums. He performed all over the United States and Europe."

"What about your parents?"

"My grandmother had eight children. My mother only had me. She made her career as a singer. A leading record label, Fania All Stars, signed a contract with her for ten albums ahead, so she wouldn't go off to their competitors. We lived in a smart house in the suburbs. My mother divorced my father—she was very independent. She lived life to the full. And the older I got, the harder it was for me to come to terms with reality . . ."

"Meaning?"

"With inequality. With the fact that some people have billions, while others have nothing. With the fact that after lessons I could go for ice cream, but thousands of children didn't even go to school. Until the revolution came. My mother was in despair. Her life was at an end. All the banquets and balls with rich entrepreneurs were over. But I felt the opposite. Even when Fidel took away our house and all our furniture, I believed he was doing the right thing."

"Do you really think so?"

"Of course. Ours is the only country where people are truly equal."

"But poor."

"There's poverty everywhere. But equality only exists here, in our country. The revolution is the love of my life, second only to salsa. I dance for Fidel. I pin beautiful flowers in my hair and paint my fingernails for him. Look, the longest one I have is painted in the colors of the Cuban flag."

"Have you ever been abroad?"

"Not until I turned sixty, when I went to dance at promotional events for the Buena Vista Social Club albums. It was a great experience—the plane journey, the smart hotels, the meetings with musicians. We danced in London, Vienna, and Zurich. The boys from Buena Vista are our friends. They arranged the trip. Ibrahim Ferrer used to spend hours at our apartment. Whenever he had a fight with his wife, he'd come over to our place with a bottle of rum, drink it all himself and stay for the night. Unfortunately, later on he earned a lot of money, bought a big house outside Havana, and pretended not to know us. And then he died."

"Money changes people," adds Oswaldo. "We earn just the right amount—it's enough to live on. We give plenty to the state— a license to run a business costs a few hundred pesos, equivalent to about fifteen dollars. We can't afford to swap this apartment for anything bigger. This room is one hundred and thirty square feet. Not so long ago there were five of us living here. Luckily, the children moved out. It's a good thing we don't have to give them extra money."

"I gave birth to six children. This stallion here did that for me," she laughs, pointing at her husband. "Every time, two weeks after the birth I was dancing again. Dancing is my entire life. Dancing and the revolution."

The German businessman: I'll sell them anything

By the road near Ciego de Ávila, a colonial gem full of horse-drawn cabs, stands a four-by-four. Raised on a jack, it has red registration plates, just like our Peugeot. Michael, a German of about sixty, is struggling with a punctured tire. He wasn't provided with a spare wheel at the rental place. So I pick him up in my car and help him find a tire shop.

Michael is pretending to be someone he's not. Officially, he came as a tourist, to stay at a resort. Unofficially, he's a businessman looking for contacts.

"Cuba's a blank page," he explains. "The analysis says that after Castro's death there might be a change of course to socialism with elements of the free market. Quarter capitalism. Apparently, the younger ministers and officers are exerting a lot of pressure on Raúl. They didn't fight in the revolution and its ethos is alien to them. They just want to earn more money and improve their standard of living."

"And then what?"

"If Cuba opens up to the world, you'll be able to sell them anything. There's a lack of clothing, cars, furniture, food. Whatever you import here, you'll sell. Panties? You'll sell 'em. Canned food? That too. Chairs? You'll sell them. Teddy bears? Those too. They're half a century behind the rest of the world! It'll be real good business!"

"So what are you doing here?"

"I'm looking for someone who could be a rep for my firm. I'm taking down the details of black-market money changers, hotel con men, cigar sellers, and the like. That's how my colleagues made contacts in Poland. I was there with them a few times."

"In Poland?"

"Sure! Cuba generally reminds me of the late Communist era

in Poland. The same dependencies between services and business. Lines outside the hard-currency shops and the ordinary stores. Lots of uncertainty, but with hope for a better future."

"So, what's your biggest problem?"

"Getting through to the services. If there ever is a transformation in Cuba, they'll be behind it. Without them, it'll be impossible to invest here. Each day I call up my wife and say I'm looking for the golden boys. I hope they're bugging the goddamn phone. And that they'll come forward of their own accord."

I have no way of verifying Michael's stories. Believe him or not, I help him change the wheel that's been fixed at the tire shop; then we say good-bye and I set off back to Varadero.

A year after Fidel's death

McDonald's has already signed a contract with the Cuban government—a year after Fidel's death, it's going to open its first restaurant in Havana. It'll be on Cathedral Square, right at the heart of Old Havana. Their hit will be the McRevolution bun, with a dash of ketchup in the shape of a red star.

Or so the people of Havana are telling each other.

II. Freedom

*For a bear, freedom is such a shock that you can't
just let it out of a cage and into the woods. You have
to give it a few days to adapt. Freedom means new
challenges. New sounds. New smells. New food.
For them, freedom is one big adventure.*

Poland / United Kingdom: Lady Peron

Victoria coach station, central London. It's midnight, and the station has been taken over by people with nowhere to go: the homeless, the jobless, beggars, vagrants, and derelicts. A curious trio has gathered on the small seats in the waiting room—a plastered punk, a well-dressed guy, and an old woman with a shopping cart of the sort homeless people sometimes have. The woman is calmly making herself supper. The men have homed in on her like chicks surrounding a mother hen.

"You're our station granny!" the punk bellows at her. "You're our station granny!"

The woman stops slicing the bread to yell back, in Polish, "You brat, I'm not a granny! I'm only fifty-five! I am Lady Peron! It's high time you got it right!" *Peron* is the Polish word for a station platform.

But the youth has his own ideas. He stands up, rather unsteadily, and tries to give Granny a kiss. He gets a smack in the mouth, a backhander, with the palm open.

"You're a good granny," he drools. "Just like the real thing. If you need comfort, she gives it to you. And if you need a smack in the gob, she can give you that too."

"Get lost, you brat, you drunk! I haven't the strength to put up with you!" shouts the woman. "They'll kill me here—they'll do me in! I'll jump off a bridge! Go buy me a lemon, would you? And a pound of sugar," she says, quite calmly turning to the smart guy.

The Lady's kingdom

Long, long ago, the Lady lived in an old cottage outside Pabianice, a town in central Poland, and her only knowledge of large train stations and foreign capital cities came from the newspapers. She would cut out the more interesting articles and pictures, and keep them as souvenirs. In those days her name was Alicja, just as it says on her ID card.

She still has the clippings to this day. For instance, there's one about the time the controversial, anti-EU politician Andrzej Lepper met Pope John Paul II. And there's one about the London bus that was ripped apart by a terrorist bomb. When she cut them out, she can't possibly have imagined that in the near future buses just like that one would be waking her up at night. Or that she herself would be accused of terrorism.

In the days when she cut out the Lepper clipping, she was still living in the Polish countryside. She never made it to the traveling store in time. Everything had always been bought up before she could drag herself all the way there.

She cut out the article about the bus when she was living at the station in Koluszki, where there's a major railroad junction. But even then she had no idea how nicely it would all turn out.

These days her estate is a rectangle two hundred by fifty yards in size—two acres. "Over there's Victoria, here's Coach, and there's Green Line too, the one you arrive at from Poland," she says, pointing, as if showing which type of crop grows where.

Victoria is a large railroad station. Coach and Green Line are bus stations. For five months, she has been lady of the manor here. She has no roof over her head, so the rectangle between the stations is her home. She has no refrigerator, so the station supermarkets are her cold store. She has no money, but she takes handouts.

The Lady at Koluszki station

"How did you end up here, ma'am?" I ask.

"Poverty drove me away from home," she explains. "In Poland I wouldn't have a cottage anymore. The laths were all rotten. The wind had damaged the rafters. Everything needed replacing. I applied to the local authority, but all they said was, 'There's nothing we can do.' That tipped the balance, because I did have some money—a monthly allowance of five hundred zlotys (then about US$125). It was enough to live on. But I was freezing in my own cottage. When I realized that I might die of cold, I packed a bag, then a second one, and went to the station."

"What sort of station?"

"The railroad station."

"And took the train to London?" I say in surprise.

"Not as quickly as that," laughs the Lady. "First I slept at the station in Piotrków, then at Koluszki. But it wasn't too bad in Poland, because I slept in the waiting room. Not like here, on a bench or on the sidewalk. The only thing I didn't like in Poland was that the station bums drink methylated spirits. And they make a dreadful stink, because they piss and crap and smoke cigarettes. Those people are the dregs of society, as low as you can get. If they're going to drink, they should drink wine or vodka. That's what civilized people do."

The Lady has a bit of a thing about etiquette. Although everyone, old and young, calls each other by their first name at Victoria station, she doesn't let them do it to her. There has to be respect!

"But did you just come straight to London from the station at Koluszki?" I ask, still in the dark.

"No, first there was Strasbourg. Meaning what, you ask? Come on, they're closing."

Indeed, the clock has struck one, and Coach is closing for the night. The Lady dutifully gathers up her bits of bread and wraps her Podlaski meat paste (given to her by a Pole) in plastic. "There's no talking to these fellows in the yellow coats," she explains, slowly getting up. "How much grief they've given me, how many tears I've shed! Twice I've been in the hospital thanks to them! I want to tell the whole of England about it. They manhandle me and throw me out. I tumble over, and they're after me. But I'm a cripple—I'm quite incapable of working!"

I help her to push her cart. Slowly we emerge into the street.

"We're going over there. Nowadays I sleep in that doorway," she says, pointing out an office block, fifty yards from the station. "First I slept behind the bus shelter. But it's windy there. My lower back, my lumbago, is making itself felt, because I've caught a chill sleeping on concrete."

There's justice in Strasbourg

"Fifteen acres and a good many square feet of land. That's dandy—don't you think?" asks the Lady, to be sure.

That's how much land the neighbors stole from her mother. "Daddy had left us," she explains. "If he'd been living with us, they'd never have taken it. But as it was, there was no farmer, so no one to defend it. My mother was an even worse cripple than I am. She'd prop her leg on a low stool and just sit there—she couldn't stand. I used to wait on her. When I was younger I could manage better, but now that I'm older I've gone downhill. She died a few years ago."

After her mother's death, as she tells the story, her neighbors started to have designs on her land and her cottage. They wanted to send her to a shelter. "'Over my dead body,' I said to myself!" says the Lady, getting emotional. "I read in the paper that Strasbourg is the seat of justice. That Strasbourg helps people who are cheated by the Polish state. So I bought a ticket, and off I went to Strasbourg."

"How do you mean?"

"Quite normally. I boarded the bus and off I went. I thought they might give me a place to live there. I wanted to live there, because it's a warm country. And I wanted to sue for that piece of land."

"Weren't you afraid?"

"I was dreadfully afraid! Before then, the farthest I'd ever been was to Łódź. And to my job in Pabianice. I was a machine knitter—I made the linings for gloves. It's hard work, because you do it standing up. And once I started getting an allowance instead, I never went outside my village at all. It's a godforsaken place! But in those days I was afraid to go anywhere, because a person's greatest fear is when he goes away for the first time. So in those days I used to think, 'Should I go or not? Unless I meet a Pole, I won't be able to communicate there!' And that's just what happened. I was crying like a baby in the street. A girl and her boyfriend stopped. She took me by the arm and showed me the way to the great big tribunal. And there, one of those men who stand in the doorway said, 'Why did you come here? People don't come to us! They write!'"

"What about the people in your village? What did they say?"

"When I told them I was going to Strasbourg to appeal, they laughed and tapped at their foreheads. They said I'd never get anything sorted out. And they were right about that, because I failed to fix anything at all."

"So was it worth going there?"

"Yes, because I saw how easy it all is. Everywhere people helped me, drove me, asked me what I needed. And I thought, maybe it's always like this; maybe wherever I go, someone's always going to help a cripple. And one time I was standing at the station when a gentleman came by and gave me two euros. I only had to hold out my hand, and people started giving me money, just like that! I thought, 'I should go back there one day.'"

A few months went by. Instead of Strasbourg, the Lady set off for London.

"They told me this place was swarming with Poles. And it's true. There are more Poles here than English people. I meet wonderful people, who help me a lot. One of them paid for me to have a hotel room, two nights for thirty pounds each. I've got the hotel bill as a memento. Another one gave me a blanket and a nice big pillow. And there's a doctor who comes by now and then for a chat and brings me something to eat. Dear God, how happy I am to have met them! To begin with, I was scared I'd meet nothing but bums, drunks, and vagrants. 'Granny', they call, 'give us a quid or two for a cider.' I'm supposed to fund you, am I? When you're so pickled you're about to keel over? Like hell I am!"

"Ded" means death

The journey to the doorway takes us fifteen minutes. The most difficult obstacle is the curb. It's too high. Lady Peron takes very small steps—each one causes her pain. She's felt this pain since childhood. "I can't do a thing. Stand still, or lift things—I keep falling over," she explains. "My legs hurt immediately. And I've had it from birth. I was born a cripple. I've got one leg an inch and a half shorter and a crooked pelvis. My parents only took me to the doctor in the second year at junior school. An infant would have recovered at once. But as it was, my bones were too old."

We're there at last. The Lady paces anxiously from corner to corner. She has to find a niche where it won't be windy. And she does, right by the entrance. But minutes later, a young black woman from the security team appears and shoos us out of the doorway. "This lady is homeless," I explain.

"If you don't go away from here, I'll have to call the police," replies the security woman, although she plainly feels stupid saying it. She offers to go and get a sandwich or a mug of tea for the Lady, but there's no question of letting her sleep in the doorway.

"I am an IN-VA-LID!" explains the Lady. It doesn't work. "I'll kill myself. I'll jump in the river or throw myself under a train!"

Nothing doing. The security woman vanishes. The Lady looks at me in admiration. "You speaky the English very nice. Quickly. But for me it's better if I don't understand. Sometimes they just give up—'I can't get through to the old girl, so let her sleep there if she must.'"

"Don't you know any English at all?" I ask.

"I can manage a few words, but not much. I can say "pliss, woter hot." That means 'hot water, please.' "Pliss, woter kold"— that's 'cold water, please.' "Gud monink," "gud nait," and "gud bai." And when they chase me away, I say, "ded." "Ded" is death. I'll die here in London—you'll finish me off. If you won't let me collect a little money, I'll die of starvation."

Pliss geev mi manny

Lady Peron sits on a suitcase. The cart is next to her, and there's a piece of paper on the ground. "I am homeless and crippled," it says. "Please help. Thank you very much"—written in English by the Poles at the bus station. She doesn't like begging. Anyway, is it begging? It's a request for help. "I don't go up to people. I'm ashamed to. I just sit here, and if someone wants to make a donation, it's voluntary. But the police harass me. They take away my sign and say, 'That's not legal here!'

"One time I lost my temper. Because there were some fellows at the railroad station dressed in capes, collecting money in a yellow bucket, the sort you fill with herrings. Apparently, some misfortune had befallen them. And I said to the policemen, 'So when they beg, it's legal, but when I do, it's not?'

"The policemen still drove me away, so then I went up to the man with the bucket. 'If you please,' I say, 'pliss geev mi manny.' Boldly, just like that. But he didn't respond at all! So I tried again: 'geev mi manny, am poor.' That had an effect on him. He gave me a pound."

The best place to beg is at the entrance to the underground station. Unfortunately, that's where they drive you away the quickest. "People were very nice and generous there," says the Lady dreamily. "I got twenty pounds in half an hour. There were black people who went by, and yellow ones too. If I'd stopped there a few hours, I'd have had a hundred pounds!"

The British are afraid of bombs

We cross to the other side of the street, where there's an emergency exit from the station. The Lady has never slept here before, but why not give it a try? "As long as they don't wake me up in the morning. Because I like to sleep in until nine or ten."

There's a good spot near the bars, but there's a guy who sometimes sleeps there. "I'm afraid to go near him, because a fellow might suddenly get ideas about sex into his head," explains the Lady.

But the exit from the station is all right too—it's sheltered from the wind. I help the Lady to carry her cart up the steps, and at once she starts unpacking her belongings.

"Look, mister, I got myself a nice cart, didn't I?" she reminds herself. "I used to pull along a suitcase on a sort of luggage trolley. I hired it at the rail station. You put in a pound and pull it along."

"Was that when you were accused of terrorism?"

"No, that was later on. When I took another trolley. The police took me to the police station, because they'd seen a knife. I used it to butter my bread. They locked me in a cell for six hours. They thought I was a terrorist. They were terrified by the trolley. They thought I had a bomb. They thought I'd leave the trolley, then go away, and a bomb would blow up. They're terrified of bombs!" She laughs. "If not for the ripiter"—that's the interpreter—"they'd have locked me up for several years."

Lady Peron pulls the quilt right up to her nose.

Or maybe Majorca?

Next day we have arranged to meet at the coach station. The Lady has dug her greatest treasures out of the shopping cart to show me. The ticket to Strasbourg, a hotel receipt (thirty pounds for the night plus breakfast), photos of a medic, the cottage outside Pabianice, and some newspaper clippings. She's been collecting them since she was a little girl.

"I collect articles about floods, and where someone got married or was born. As a reminder that those events took place."

Among the clippings is the most important one, about Strasbourg. And one about Alicja herself, from *Życie Pabianic*, Pabianice's local newspaper. She doesn't like it, because the journalist ridiculed her journey to Strasbourg.

"But you'll write seriously about me—won't you, mister?" she asks me.

"Of course," I assure her.

"You'll write that I travel about the world despite being a cripple from birth?"

"Yes."

"And maybe give an address. In case people want to send me some money, eh?"

But it's hard to give an address for the Lady. In London she lives in the street, and she'll only spend a few days in Poland. "There will be four months' pension money waiting. I'll get two thousand at once, and I'll have the money to go to Italy. Or Majorca. That's just beyond Spain. If I'm going to be homeless and alone, I might as well be somewhere that's warm. That's what I've been thinking lately."

The Lady puts on a pair of dark glasses. Not on her eyes but on her hair. "This is how the smart young ladies wear them," she explains to me. "I'm not a smart young lady, but you have to look nice for a photo."

I take a few snaps.

Then the Lady asks me to do her a favor. She wants me to nip over to Victoria and buy her a big bag of fries and two piña coladas. "It's a very light little drink," she says, smiling.

The fries must be from a particular place—the ones they make there are soft, and the Lady has hardly any teeth. I'm back in half an hour. The Lady looks as if she's been at a standstill in the meantime. Neither her face, nor the position of her body have budged at all. She's clearly brilliant at freezing on the spot. She wakes up at my arrival.

"Would you please explain, why do they refuse to give me an apartment?" asks the Lady, and gives her own answer. "Because the state is very greedy. If it has a lot, it wants even more. What do they do with all the money? They never have enough. Once they've got Europe, they want the entire globe. The rich don't know what poverty means, and all my life I've never known what it means to be rich."

Suddenly the Lady falls silent, smiles, and takes me by the arm.

"But tell me frankly, mister. Many a healthy person hasn't seen as much of the world as this cripple from Pabianice."

III. Negotiations

*The handover has to be prepared a long way in
advance . . . . These things take months to negotiate.
You have to sit down at the table with them once,
twice, a third time, to make friends and gain each
other's trust. Without mutual trust none of them
would hand over his bear. They'd sooner kill it.*

Ukraine: Nothing Bleeps for the Smugglers

I'm sitting in the passenger seat of a six-year-old Passat, and my
heart is in my mouth. I'm chain-smoking, nervously looking
around me, and sending off my final text messages.

A few days ago I met Marek (not his real name), a young man
of my age, from a Polish village on the Ukrainian border. As we
drank hooch together, Marek admitted that he takes cars across
the border. Not entirely legally. He exploits the fact that in
Ukraine the customs duty on used cars from the West is often
more than they're worth, but he knows how to get a car across the
border—either without paying any customs duty at all or only
paying the minimum. How does he do it? He'll tell me on the
way, because he's taking me with him.

"Are you up for it, Ed?" asked Marek. "Ed" is short for "editor."

"Sure I am," I replied.

And now I've got what I deserve.

Marek drives over to fetch me two days later, and now we're at the border, sitting in the Passat bought by a friend of his in Switzerland for a few thousand euros. I can see a customs officer, a border guard, flags—Poland and the European Union, a bridge with the Bug River below it, and a barrier, the point of no return, getting nearer and nearer.

The driver: Putin won't let us join

As we sit in a line of cars on the bridge marking the border, the diplomats in Brussels are contemplating how to move that border farther away. In short, how to encourage Ukraine to adopt reforms and ultimately join the EU. Or at least connect up with it for good.

We don't yet know that very soon President Viktor Yanukovych is going to show the EU the finger, and the Ukrainians are going to mobilize for weeks and weeks of pro-EU demonstrations, which will end with the death of dozens of demonstrators; as a result, Yanukovych will flee from Ukraine.

We don't yet know that soon after that Vladimir Putin will cut off the Crimean peninsula from Ukraine.

But there's one thing the Ukrainians I speak to know all too well: their entry into the EU isn't going be along a path strewn with roses.

"We're never going to join the EU," says Alexander, a driver approaching the barrier in a van packed with people. His passengers are on their way home from seasonal work in Poland—they've been picking strawberries, then raspberries, then potatoes, and lastly apples and plums. "The season's over, so the people are going home," says Alexander. "Some of them are still there—they're taking mushrooms to the purchase point, but that's just for small change. What about the EU? First and foremost, Putin will never let us join it. For him, Ukraine is part of Russia, and that's that. He'll never agree to hand us over to the West," he says, and the Ukrainians coming home from seasonal labor agree. "Anyway, Donbas, or eastern Ukraine, would be happy to join Russia. They speak Russian there, and to this day they're still weeping for the USSR, saying what a wonderful country it was, where everyone had a job. But the fact that in the Soviet days, in the 1930s, Stalin starved ten million Ukrainians to death doesn't interest them anymore!"

"My great-grandmother died during the Great Famine," says an older man in a cap, nodding. "My name is Alexander Khodukin, and I used to work as a stoker at the cultural center, but now I'm retired. My mother told me that in the 1930s people ate earth and each other to survive. Mothers suffocated their own children so they wouldn't suffer. Dreadful times. Russia has never apologized for it, and now they're threatening that if we sign an agreement with the EU, they'll starve us again as a punishment. They'll close the border so we won't be able to buy or sell anything, and they'll also double or triple the price we pay for gas."

The priest: the EU is Satan

Father Oleg Azarenkov has a graying beard, hair tied in a ponytail, and an unstylish acrylic sweater. He's driving an old Lada, and when it comes to joining the EU, he worked out his opinion long ago. "The thought fills me with horror."

For seventeen years, Father Oleg has been in service at a small wooden church in a village called Bila, not far from the Russian border. For half that time, he has been embroiled in a feud.

"When the orange rabble came to power ten years ago, they told me to share my church with Filaret's lot," he complains. "My God, how much grief I've had because of them!"

"Filaret's lot" are those faithful to the Kiev Patriarchate, which is at loggerheads with the Moscow Patriarchate. Their leader is Patriarch Filaret.

The "orange rabble" are the politicians who came to power thanks to the Orange Revolution. But why does Father Oleg from the Moscow Patriarchate call them "the rabble"?

"Witold, what on earth did they think they were doing? They said that every other day I'll take the service in the church, and the rest of the time their priest will do it. To me, he's just an ordinary layman. So they came along, broke the locks, put on a new chain, and for several years I had no key to my own church! Luckily, since Yanukovych has been the president, things have calmed down a bit, and at least they've given me back the keys. As for the EU, we can't expect anything good from that direction."

"But a few weeks ago all Ukraine's religious leaders signed a letter in support of Ukraine joining the EU," I say. "It was signed by the patriarch of your church as well as by Filaret, Father."

"I'll tell you something, Witold," says Father Oleg, frowning. "The patriarch has to be a bit of a politician, so he says and signs various things. But we, the ordinary priests, had a meeting in Kiev a year ago to talk about the EU. A lady came from France and told us very nicely about the money they're going to give us for renovating churches, about the grants we'll get. And she showed us some slides: from France, Belgium, and Poland. We listened, until one of the older priests got up and said, 'Your churches may well have been beautifully restored. They may have copper on the roofs and marble on the floors. Our churches are often just made of plywood, and their foundations are collapsing. But our churches are full—yours are empty.' And we all began to applaud, because it's the truth. The West has forgotten about God—it's all too apparent among you Poles. Ever since you joined the EU, your country is richer and richer. Just across the border everything's nicely paved. But a man who is rich soon forgets about God—he's too busy wheeling and dealing to increase his wealth. And the man who forgets about God immediately forgets about other people too. Unfortunately, it's plain to see in your country. Two years ago I drove across Poland to Germany with the little mother . . ."

"With whom?"

"With my wife. On the way, our car broke down. We waved for two hours, but nobody stopped. Nobody wanted to help us, though I was standing by the road in my cassock, wearing my cross. They just pointed at us, as if it were a great show. The only people who stopped to help when they saw that we were in trouble were a Ukrainian couple."

"That could happen anywhere."

"That's nothing. What worries me most is that the EU will attack us with sex—they'll tell us to change the law to protect perverts! You'll be able to go about Kiev like Adam and Eve in paradise. And a man will be able to kiss a man. In the Holy Scriptures it says that sort of behavior heralds the Apocalypse. And do you know the Pochayiv monastery, the most sacred site in western Ukraine? Did you know that people who are possessed by devils go there? And did you know that recently the devil entered a man when he was reading a brochure about that EU of yours? They took him to Pochayiv, and the devil inside him spat at the priests, and said it was on its way to Ukraine, that it was already here. And that the politicians were providing it with a carriage. All evil comes from the West, Witold."

The smuggler: our guys only take large bribes

The line moves at a sluggish rate; every few minutes we drive forward about thirty feet. This has been going on for more than an hour and will continue for at least twice as long.

Marek is wearing a leather jacket, a turtleneck sweater, and good quality jeans. He also has a Diesel shirt and an expensive-looking watch. He smells sophisticated, of Dior aftershave. He looks like a cross between a petty con man and someone who aspires to a slightly larger world.

"Everything matters on the border, even how you dress," he explains to me. "Every Ukrainian customs official is a mini psychologist. If you look too rich, they'll have you give them more of a bribe, because you've gotten too big. If you look too poor, they won't want to talk to you. We have to be careful not to go too far either way. They all know each other here. When one of my pals did well and bought himself a brand-new Audi, the Ukrainians stopped letting him take cars through. And it wasn't about income but principles."

"Meaning?"

"They know that in their corner of hell they'll never earn as much as we do. We sometimes meet up with them privately for a barbecue and a drink. They don't live too badly. But they say that to get into the Ukrainian customs service, you've got to bring in twenty thousand dollars just for starters. And then each month you have to give the boss his cut. Three years in the job and you've got to contribute another twenty thousand or they'll throw you out. So they take two zlotys from each old lady with two packs of cigarettes. And they take five from every old man who's carrying petrol. Because they have to bring in that twenty thousand as fast as they can."

"But do you know that for sure?"

"Well, I've never caught them in the act," says Marek, frowning. "I'm just repeating what they told me."

"What about the Polish customs officials? Do they take bribes?"

"Not from us. To them we're retailers. If they do, it's solid cash, for a whole truckload of cigarettes. Besides, they don't have a problem with letting a car out of Poland, if all the papers are in order."

"And are they?"

"Do I look like some kind of Balkan greaser who goes around stealing cars?" says Marek indignantly. "The exchange rate is good enough for us to ship cars we've bought legally. I bought this one in Germany for just under five thousand euros. I'll make another two thousand on it, but I'll share out more than half of that with the guys. These people here on the border are going to get some cash now. Then the police across the border will get some too, and at the end of the month I'll go have a drink with them and leave them a bit more. Even after that I'll be left with twenty thousand zlotys for my own needs. How much do you earn, Ed? How much?! The drivers working for me get more than that. I could pass the occasional job your way. Then you'd earn a bit of extra—what do you say?"

The husband: he doesn't feel like it

Yevheniya Cherniak cleans under Polish beds, washes Polish dishes, irons Polish shirts, and makes dinners out of Polish meat and potatoes. Every few months she makes a trip home to her village in Volhynia, western Ukraine. This time she's traveling with a friend who's going to visit his mother in the hospital. Both our Passat and their Fiat Ducato have already passed the Polish border point. Together we're waiting to enter Ukraine.

Yevheniya has streaks in her hair and wrinkles on her face. But she looks younger than her sixty years of age. "The European Union? I like it very much," she says dreamily. "The best thing is that nowadays when I get a visa to Poland, I can go and see my daughter in Berlin on the same visa. Poland is now a fully fledged European country. I've seen all this change happening with my own eyes. I've been going to and fro like this for twelve years now. Take clothes, for example. I remember when the Poles went about dressed like in the Soviet Union. They'd just toss on any old thing and leave the house. But nowadays the women are like out of a fashion magazine. Even the men are starting to take care of themselves. When I'm cleaning the bathrooms, more and more often I see special men's toiletries.

"In the old days, when I was at my daughter's place in Berlin I could recognize a Pole instantly in the street. I could see who was from our part of the world, from the East. But now, until I hear them speak, I can't tell. You Poles are looking better. And you're eating better too. These days every Biedronka supermarket sells olive oil. And Italian cheese. And Parma ham. Everyone goes to Poland for their shopping, because in Ukraine, even though we've got the best earth in Europe, it lies fallow. You tell me, Witold, where's the sense in that? Ukraine could be Europe's granary. You could eat our black earth with a spoon—there's no soil like it anywhere in the world. But what happens? It just lies fallow. People are only interested in opportunities to earn money abroad. Or to get something for nothing, just as they got used to doing under the Commies. My old man doesn't meet any of the EU standards. He's never seen face cream in his life. Whatever cash I send him, he drinks away. I keep telling him: 'We were given two and a half acres when they closed down the collective farm. You could take just a little bit of it and sow some carrots, cucumbers, and tomatoes. You could raise hens. Why not have something of your own?'"

"And what does he say to that?"

"He says he won't do it! Because he doesn't feel like it. Unfortunately, the whole Ukrainian nation is just like our marriage. Either they work hard, but abroad, like me. Or they sit in their village and whack a stick against a tree in the hope that a pear might fall. I pray for the EU to come to us too. For the Dutch and the Germans to come here, and the Poles too, and plough that land for us. The collective farm will start up again, but this time it'll be privately owned."

The shift leader: you can drive on

Right behind our Passat there's an ancient Zaporozhets—a Soviet-era car—that could easily be put on show in a motor museum. It's spitting out small black clouds of exhaust. Inside there's an old couple: Gramps is wearing a beret with a little stalk, and Granny's in a headscarf. "Small fry," says Marek, scowling. "They've got two rings of sausage and a six-pack of yogurts. And a tankful of gasoline—of course, they've probably got extra fuel tanks in the wheel arches. They'll only make thirty zlotys out of it, but that'll top up their pension."

In front of us there's a fifteen-year-old Golf, driven by a young man with a shaved head. "Oh, he's a pal of mine. Hey, Vova, what you carrying?" Marek jovially addresses the bald guy.

"What's it got to do with you?" asks Vova with a lilting eastern accent.

"He's small fry too," says Marek, winking at me. "They're all smuggling sausage and cheese. Every other car has some sort of hiding place—in the door, the roof, or the floor. They bring smokes our way and go back with chow, because in Ukraine everything's pricier and worse quality than in Poland."

We drive forward another ten yards. By now there's a blue-and-yellow Ukrainian flag looming in the distance. Finally, we get right up to it.

"This is where it starts to happen, Ed. Watch carefully," says Marek, then smiles broadly, shouts, *"Dobroho dnia!"*—Ukrainian for "good day"—to the customs official, and presses something into his hand.

"Was that a bribe?" I ask.

"Noooo, just a little gift."

It turned out that was just the start of the gift giving. Marek is on first-name terms with all the border guards and customs officials. Even the shift leader comes over to give him a high five.

"So who's this?" he asks, pointing a finger at me.

"A pal. He's learning," says Marek, laughing.

"The shift leaders are the wiliest of all," he says later. "They don't accept the gifts with their own hands—they have people to do that for them. And if things were to fall apart—the inspectors do occasionally come from Kiev—the lower ranking guy's to blame."

Indeed, once the shift leader has gone, the customs officials take the money quite openly. They're not particularly bothered that people can see everything. Marek gives them two fat rolls of banknotes. "I could give them a fifty-euro note each, but there's psychology at work here too," he says. "If he gets a wad of banknotes, he feels as if he's got a lot of cash. If he only got one, he'd be less satisfied."

"And what are you actually paying them for, if the car's aboveboard?"

"The fact that I've entered the country by car is peanuts. But they're supposed to enter it in their system—I drove in by car, so I should be leaving by car too. If I don't have a car on my way out of Ukraine, their computer should start to bleep. If I'm not going back in it, I should be presenting a certificate of sale or write-off in Ukraine. Otherwise they can't let me out."

"But they will?"

"We're going to go back, and then you'll see if the computer bleeps."

The client: Brussels will reduce us to penury

About seven miles from the border, in a woodland roadhouse by a small lake, the client is already waiting for us. His name is Alyosha and he's got a stylish shirt, an expensive watch, and a silver Lexus. A driver gets into our Passat to take it on farther.

"It's going all the way to Odessa," says Alyosha in broken Polish, taking some money out of a leather wallet. "Well, boys, you must excuse me, but I can't chat. My next car's coming in an hour, at the other crossing. I've got fifty miles ahead of me. I must dash."

"Off you run, Alyosha. Maybe by the next time we meet you'll be in the European Union," jokes Marek.

"Shut the fuck up about your European Union," says Alyosha, scowling. "God forbid it ever gets here, or they'll even up the customs duty and we'll both be reduced to penury!" He fires up the Lexus.

"It might reduce him, but not me," smiles Marek.

We finish our lunch and set off back to Poland with Andrzej, a colleague of Marek's who has come specially to fetch us. "A few years ago I bought a piece of land not far from the new border crossing at Budomierz," Marek tells me. "I have two and a half acres, quite near the road. I might open a shop there, or a pub, or maybe a supermarket. European Union or not, you can always carve a slice at the border."

We recross the border just before nightfall. We hand over

our passports for clearance. Once again I've got my heart in my mouth and am chain-smoking.

But the young customs official sends us off without batting an eyelid. Nothing bleeps.

The old age pensioner: may I die before the Union

Valentina Kalennikova is standing at a small bazaar by the exit from the border crossing in Medyka, between a pizzeria and a parking lot. In one hand she's wielding two packs of Paramount cigarettes, one of the cheapest brands, and in the other a bottle of vodka with a wholesome-looking ear of wheat on the label. She's on the hunt for a customer.

"I've got a good eye for people," she says. "I'm almost eighty now, so I don't run up to the cars as quickly as the younger women. But I seem to have a sense of who's going to buy and where to position myself. Besides, the younger girls give me space. They know it's not so easy for an old granny to stand here all day. In exchange, I say prayers and light candles for them in the church."

Mrs. Kalennikova is legally entitled to take two packs of cigarettes and a bottle of vodka into Poland. She sells the cigarettes for four zlotys each and the vodka for ten. Like this, she earns her first thirty hryvnia (there were then about eight hryvnia to the dollar).

And she'll get a few more hryvnia for getting into a car that's carrying a washing machine or other white goods across the border. You can only take one item per person, so drivers who are transporting several at a time have to take extra people with them. How many washing machines have been driven into Ukraine thanks to Mrs. Kalennikova by now? God alone knows.

On the one hand, Mrs. Kalennikova has heard that the EU will open up the border. That would be good. She wouldn't have to wait in line for over an hour, day in, day out, in snow and rain. She wouldn't have to go through under the vigilant eye of the customs officials and EU scanners that cost millions of euros, there to judge whether she's carrying more than two packs and one bottle.

On the other hand, what if the price of cigarettes goes up? In Poland they have, and dramatically so. "I might just as well dig myself a grave," says Mrs. Kalennikova. And she starts to cry.

"Don't cry, Granny," the younger women say. "Even if we do join the European Union, you won't be on this earth anymore. We'll be the ones to worry about it."

They're right, so Mrs. Kalennikova adjusts the knot in her headscarf and runs off to find her next customer for a pack of Paramount cigarettes.

IV. History

The Bulgarian Gypsies say the females are easier to train—they're less aggressive and don't attack people. But the Polish Gypsies regarded the training of the females as dishonorable. In their view the females should bear young, so the keepers will never lack bears for their work.

Albania: The End of the Concrete Toadstools

First of all you pack old tires around the bunker and set them alight. Or you put a sack of agricultural fertilizer with a high potassium content inside it. That makes a primitive bomb, and the bunker blows up.

"All to make the concrete crack," explains Djoni, a construction worker from Berat in central Albania. "Once it cracks, we whack it with hammers to get to the steel that's inside. There can be as much as two tons of it—half a pound earns you fifteen (euro) cents at the recycling center. So from one bunker you can make three hundred euros! That's a lot of money in Albania, especially when it's literally just lying on the ground. But sometimes you have to keep at it for a whole five days to make the concrete crack. And my boss, the owner of the construction firm where I work, takes most of the money anyway. I earn about twenty to thirty euros per bunker."*

1.

But Djoni's not complaining. He couldn't have chosen a better job. For the past few years Albania has been having a construction boom that has inflated the price of steel, which hasn't even been halted by the crisis in Italy and Greece, where hundreds of thousands of Albanian immigrants work. In fact, the experts are warning that this boom is really just a cover to suit the needs of the Italian Mafia, which is laundering its dirty money by building tower blocks that no one in Albania needs—in some of them more than half the apartments are empty. But the Albanians take no notice of that.

"The crisis isn't being felt here in Albania," stresses Djoni. "Our prime minister boasted that apart from Albania, the only other country in Europe that isn't in recession is Poland—our growth rate for 2011 was over 3 percent."

Djoni also worked in Greece for several years, at Piraeus, but he got fed up with playing blindman's buff with the local border guards, who regularly catch Albanians working illegally. "My health's not what it was," he says. "Here I earn less, but I spend less too. It comes out about the same."

So during the day, Djoni builds new housing developments, and in the evenings he tops up his salary by demolishing bunkers.

---

* In 2012 one euro was worth US$0.77. So while there was three hundred euros to be made from a bunker (US$231), Djoni was only earning the equivalent of US$15–23 for each one.

Thanks to the money he has earned this way, he has finished building his own apartment and has sent his children to good schools.

The construction boom is one of the reasons why the Albanians have started taking notice of the hundreds of thousands of bunkers that are a blot on their landscape all the way from Shkodër on the Montenegrin border right down to Konispol, a stone's throw from Greece. Until now they have turned a blind eye to them, but now that steel has become considerably more expensive, whatever Djoni extracts from the bunkers during the night he can sell by day as reinforcing wire.

"Under Communism, I did my military training in bunkers like these," recalls Djoni. "We were taught how to camouflage them in case of attack. On the one hand, it's a part of my life, but, on the other, I don't feel sorry for them in the least bit. They're a symbol of very bad times—they should all disappear."

2.

Gjergj's bunker is painted green from top to bottom, and on the front it has a dazzling sign that says Bunker Bar. And although the beach alongside Gjergj's bar is not one of the loveliest, he's not put off. "We might not have much sand," he says, shrugging, "but we do have our concrete mushrooms, our Uncle Hoxha's toadstools. Poland hasn't got any, nor has Italy, not even Brazil. People come from all over the world to look at them!"

Gjergj invites me inside his mushroom and lets me look through the firing slit, which is aimed in the direction of Italy. And then he shows me a large, metal stick hidden in the depths.

"I used to keep it for drunken customers who don't always want to pay up," he explains. "And nowadays I keep it for the guys who come to blow up the bunkers. I've been running this bar for twelve years now, and I won't let them lay a finger on it!"

Gjergj is right about one thing—the Albanian bunkers are unique on a global scale. In a country slightly smaller than Maryland, inhabited by barely three million people, the Communists built about 750,000 of them. No one knows exactly how many there are. "Under Communism, everything to do with the bunkers was top secret—the army never published the figures. And then along came democracy. They lost the documents, and now no one's capable of counting them precisely," says Ina Izhara, a political scientist who, like many of the young people here, divides her time between Albania and Italy. "When we joined NATO a few years ago, apparently the alliance command demanded to see maps of their distribution. And consternation arose, because there weren't any maps. Someone once suggested that there are 750,000 of them, and now everyone keeps repeating that."

The fact is, the bunkers have become a permanent feature of Albania's landscape. They stand in the middle of cities and on the edge of villages, in graveyards and playgrounds; they stand on mountain tops, and half-submerged in the sea. When they plow the land, farmers often have to make a wide detour to go around them. You only have to travel by train from Tirana to Dürres to count several dozen of them, some in courtyards right next to the houses.

Elton Caushi, a tour guide from Tirana, is fascinated by them. He has worked out a route for his customers to tour the most interesting ones. "For instance, there are several of them in the ancient city of Apollonia, among the ruins left by the ancient Greeks," he says. "The tourists love them, which the Albanians can't understand."

But why on earth were these concrete mushrooms built at all? Enver Hoxha, who ruled Albania with absolute power from

1944 until his death in 1985, was afraid of being attacked by other states, both Communist and not. "He was paranoid," says Izhara. "He thought everyone wanted to invade Albania. At first, immediately after the war, he kept in with Yugoslavia. But he soon quarreled with Marshal Tito, and for a dozen years or so he teamed up with the USSR. That relationship ceased to appeal to him when they settled scores with Stalinism. So he made an alliance with China and—seeing enemies everywhere—started to arm the country to the teeth and build the bunkers."

They were an inherent part of the fears well known to the Albanians: over the centuries, Albania had been invaded and occupied by the ancient Greeks, the Romans, the Bulgarians, the Venetians, the Turks, the Italians, the Austrians, the Germans, the Serbians, and finally the modern Greeks.

"Hoxha appealed to a sensitive spot for Albanians," says Izhara. "The bunkers were built for us, rather than for foreigners—to frighten us and to instill discipline. To rule us more easily. Nowadays it might seem absurd, but people of my parents' age—now around seventy—truly believed the whole world wanted to invade us."

"The propaganda worked the way it now does in North Korea; they persuaded us that the first thing the Americans, Russians, or Greeks thought about on waking up each day was how to conquer Albania," adds Elton Caushi. "We were completely cut off from information; my uncle went to prison for twenty years because he watched a movie on Yugoslav TV and told a friend about it, who informed on him. The majority preferred not to take the risk. They listened to Radio Tirana and tried not to stick their necks out."

And so for years on end the Albanian government built fortifications rather than roads or apartments. Up to twelve people lived together in areas of five hundred square feet, because all the engineers were working for the army, and all the concrete went to build bunkers, which were never actually used for military purposes.

So what were they used for?

"We most often use them to lose our virtue," jokes Izhara. "I never had the experience, but I've heard lots of stories. Not long ago on holiday in Sarandë, a friend of mine had an adventure in a bunker with a girl he met at a disco. What was it like? He said it was awful. He got frozen to the marrow, and he ended up stepping on a turd."

3.

Hoxha died in 1985. A month before his death, Mikhail Gorbachev came to power in the Soviet Union and the winds of change began to blow in all the Communist countries—except for Albania. Here, in 1990, Hoxha's successor Ramiz Alia was still using the propaganda machine to persuade Albanians that life in Poland following the change to a capitalist system had considerably worsened.

But by then the Albanians knew their stuff. The system began to founder more and more, until in 1992 Alia handed over power to Sali Berisha, former head of the party organization at the medical academy in Tirana, who had a better sense than any of the other apparatchiks about which way the winds of history were blowing. Berisha became president, and later served as prime minister for eight years, until 2013.

But for years on end, neither he nor anyone else in power touched Hoxha's bunkers. "No one had any idea what to do with them. So it was—until 1999, when the Serbs started to bombard

Kosovo," says Caushi. "In the process Albania was hit too, and so were the bunkers. And suddenly it turned out that these structures, which were supposed to survive an atom bomb, had just fallen apart as if they were made of clay! For lots of people, it was a shock. Suddenly, they could see that the power of Communism was a matrix, a delusion, not the truth."

At that point a second civilian life began for the bunkers. People lost respect for them. In the countryside the Albanian farmers started keeping cows, goats, and pigs in them; in the cities, until recently, they served as cold stores. Now that Albania has grown rich, almost everyone has a refrigerator at home, so people have started throwing trash into the bunkers.

It's different in the capital. Blokku is a district of Tirana that in Communist times was completely closed off and guarded. This is where the bigwigs lived—Enver Hoxha, his ministers and comrades. Every building had a concrete shelter in the basement.

"These days, Blokku is the biggest rave in Tirana," jokes Kamelja, a law student. "There are several really great bars and discos in the old shelters. For people of my age, twenty-year-olds, these places have a completely different meaning than they had for our parents."

Right next to Enver Hoxha's abandoned villa, there is a trendy café and an elite English-language school. Opposite, there is a gambling arcade.

Members of the generation that only knows the bunkers as strangely shaped concrete mushrooms have been developing new uses for them. Elian Stefa, an Albanian architect of the younger generation, did his diploma project on them. "As we have to live with them, let's think up some new uses for them," he says. In his project he drew bunkers made into minihotels, and even cellars for cooling wine. "I'd be happiest of all if someone opened a hostel in a bunker," he says. "We did a visualization of what such a place could look like. Everyone likes it, but there's no one brave enough to be the first to do it."

Elton Caushi knows very well what they're talking about: "My tourists would pay anything to stay the night in something like that."

4.

In downtown Tirana there's a different bunker: it's a great big pyramid, built just after Hoxha died. It was meant to be both his tomb and a place of pilgrimage for schools, the military, and workers.

Today the pyramid is empty, covered in feeble graffiti. The bravest of the local skateboarders ride down its steep walls. "I pass it every day on my way to work," says Gjergj Ndrecën, a political prisoner in the Communist era who was locked up by Hoxha's regime for seven years for "enemy propaganda." "I just distributed a few antigovernment leaflets," says Ndrecën, who now works for a foundation that helps former political prisoners who are in a difficult financial situation. "I would have been inside for far longer if Communism hadn't collapsed. That's why every time I pass this monstrosity my blood boils. No one has ever answered for the hell they made us live in."

It's a fact. The Communists, who killed some fifty thousand people in Albania and set up reeducation camps for thousands more, have never been brought to task. Ramiz Alia died in 2011, at the age of eighty-six. A few of them did serve time in prison, but the sentences were only for abuse of power and financial fiddling, not for the crimes of the system. Toward the end of his life, the former dictator gave an interview to the BBC in which he admitted that not all the death sentences in the Communist era were justified. He said he regretted that.

The situation is different for Nexhmije Hoxha, the dictator's wife. In 2012, at age ninety-two, she appeared on a show that is extremely popular in Albania, presented by Janusz Bugajski, an American political scientist with Polish roots. During the ninety-minute conversation, she refused to show the slightest remorse. "I don't regret anything," she said. "Our country was very poor. It had lots of enemies. All those actions were necessary."

"So what should be done with the pyramid?" I ask Ndrecën.

"The same as they're doing with the bunkers! Pack it with fertilizer and tires, and set it on fire. Blowing up the bunkers is the start of our mental release from Communism. As long as we go on living in the world invented by the Communists, the spirit of Hoxha will continue to prevail here."

Will it happen? "Sure it will, as long as the price of steel stays high," says Ndrecën bitterly. "Especially since the army has started blowing them up, as well as civilians."

5.

While Djoni, the construction worker from Berat, is destroying bunkers using his own makeshift methods, the army is doing it in a much more methodical way. "They have special pneumatic drills," says Djoni, almost whistling in admiration. "Apart from that, they're allowed to fire at them from tanks and mortars. They can do as many as ten bunkers a day. That's three thousand euros! I wonder what they do with the money?" he muses.

I tried to find out all about it at the Albanian Ministry of

Defense, but my questions ran aground somewhere between departments. More facts were established by some Albanian journalists who found tanks destroying half-submerged bunkers at an Albanian tourist resort in the Seman district.

"We have to do it because they're causing whirlpools and people are being drowned," said one of the officers in charge of the operation, anonymously. "Tourists are very important for our country now."

The demolition of the bunkers proved complicated, and the army had to get help from some private construction firms. Besnik Lasku, the owner of one of them, turned out to have served in the army as a young man, and had built the bunkers.

"It brings a tear to my eye," admitted Lasku. "The bunkers are a part of my life. I never imagined that one day they'd disappear. And it feels odd to me that we're blowing them up for the sake of capitalists who are going to build expensive hotels and restaurants in their place."

V. Instincts

*We sit in our observatory and watch how they be-
have, and we work it out—how much aggression
we can allow them, whether they've already crossed
the boundary, or whether we can still give them a
while to cool down.*

Estonia: Tea with the Invader

▲▲**H**i there, my friend. Maybe you could get hold of some
TNT? There are plenty of mines in your city. We strike
like the IRA—a station or an airport. Write to my personal address. Grigori."

Sixteen-year-old Sasha received this message via Skype just
after the riots in Tallinn. When he looked up the IRA on Wikipe-
dia, he really liked what he read. "Yo, Grisha—I'll try to help," he
wrote back, and ran off to see his miner pals.

The Bronze Soldier and being pro-Moscow

Toward the end of April 2007, the Bronze Soldier of Tallinn, a memorial that symbolizes the Red Army's victory over
fascism, was moved from the city center to the outskirts.

Estonia's Russian citizens took this as a slap in the face. In

Tallinn the situation exploded. Hundreds of windows were broken and blood was shed. A young Russian was killed, and several dozen people were wounded. Thousands of hooligans, both Russian and Estonian, wrecked and looted the stores. Photos of sixteen-year-olds pillaging a Hugo Boss store went around the world.

A few days later I met up with my friend Jaan. "Goddamned Russkies," he fumed. He has spent half his life in Poland, but he always shows a lively concern for everything that's going on in his native Estonia. "Freaking fifth column! Traitors! Invaders!"

"Invaders?"

"Yes! Half of them came with the Soviet army. To keep an eye on us. So Estonia wouldn't rebel."

"Traitors?"

"They're all just waiting for the USSR to return."

"Fifth column?"

"They're plotting to join us up with Russia. Our government should send them all off to Moscow. Estonia should be Estonian."

I looked into the facts. One in three Estonian citizens is a native speaker of Russian. One in six doesn't even have Estonian citizenship. Nevertheless, Estonia is doing well, has joined the European Union, and is an economic tiger among the former Soviet republics.

"What sort of fifth column allows a country to develop like that?" I asked Jaan.

"Go and have a cup of tea from the samovar with them. You'll see for yourself how much they hate us," he replied, and broke off the conversation.

The invader and the cabbage in Kabul

While Sasha was looking for TNT, Yelena Yedomsky was given a garden plant by the Estonians she had befriended. To show their sympathy. "And we were afraid they'd stop talking to us," she told her husband.

Yelena is a therapist. Viktor is an invader. They live in a small village outside Tartu, the cultural and intellectual capital of Estonia.

The Yedomskys' neighbors are all Estonians. But they get on very well together. We're having a cup of tea, and wondering whether the Bronze Soldier might change anything here.

"The Estonians are remarkable," says Yelena with admiration. "Until 1918, they'd never had independence. They've been ruled by the Germans, the Russians, the Swedes, the Danes, and the Poles. Similar nations have died out unnoticed. Especially as they never particularly fought for independence. They just held Estonian song festivals. That was the extent of their fight."

Ever since Estonia achieved independence, Yelena and Viktor have had nothing but problems. To start with, they couldn't get citizenship. The only people with a right to an Estonian passport were citizens or the children of citizens of the First Republic, which existed from 1918 to 1940. Yelena and Viktor have lived in Estonia for almost all their lives. And yet the authorities wanted to send them off to Russia.

Says Viktor: "I might even have gone, but I have no one there. My daughters are married to Estonians. And then suddenly I find out I'm an invader."

Why is that? Because Viktor was originally sent to Estonia by Soviet air force general staff—he was a pilot.

"I flew all over the world—to China, beyond the North Pole. I was in Afghanistan. I got a ringside view of so much horror there that straight after the Afghan war I threw away my Communist Party membership card. Apparently, they spent three hours debating whether in that case they could award me a medal for valor. They did."

Viktor wears the medal on the right side of his navy-blue air force officer's uniform.

"There were Estonians serving with me. We all talked in Russian—they had only a poor command of Estonian. And suddenly in 1991 it turned out they were citizens here, and I was an invader."

"I was given an Estonian passport," says Yelena. "I stood as a candidate in the elections for the city council. It has at least been possible to stop them from deporting people like Viktor."

Nowadays Viktor has Russian citizenship with a three-year right to remain on Estonian territory. "We're afraid that because of all the unrest they'll tighten up the policy toward 'invaders,'" says Yelena. "But no way are we the fifth column! We're much better off here than we would be in Russia."

"When I went to the bazaar in Kabul with my air force pals," says Viktor, "one of the stallholders said to us in Russian, 'Good cabbage, very shitty!' Someone had taught him to prattle that nonsense. It's the same thing with the Russian youth. Someone has told them they have to defend the Bronze Soldier. So that's what they're doing."

The teacher and the Russian policemen

Everyone advised us against making a trip to Narva. Mafiosi, hired assassins, polluted air, and exploding cars. And crowds of Russians too—more than 60 percent of the population there are Russian. Some of them haven't cooled down yet since the events in Tallinn.

Even Yelena and Viktor said it was better not to go.

Day in, day out, an Estonian called Aet Kiisla had heard the same thing. Nevertheless, she accepted a job as a teacher at a college in Narva, right on the Russian border.

Before the war, the city was a jewel. Beautiful baroque houses descended down to the river's edge. The golden years were over by the end of the Second World War. Nowadays Narva is just gray high-rise blocks, with plenty of stray dogs and flocks of seagulls. In the middle of the city there's a neglected park and a "friendship bridge" clogged by a line of container trucks and a crowd of cross-border traders (known in Polish as "ants"). On the other side of the river lies the Russian city of Ivangorod.

In Narva you hear nothing but Russian—97 percent of the people are Russian. According to research, more than 60 percent of them can't speak a single word of Estonian.

Aet teaches at a college that trains other teachers for Russian-language schools. "We mainly teach in Russian. But we make it clear: 'If you want to work in this country, you have to know Estonian.' Though in a place like Narva, you can't overdo it."

"Meaning?"

"The state television is only in Estonian. That was meant to mobilize the Russians to learn it. But they watch nothing except the Russian channels. Moscow takes advantage of that and stirs things up. It persuades them that Estonia is treating them badly. And we can't offer any counterbalance. The Russians were antagonized by the Bronze Soldier because there was no way to explain it to them from our perspective."

A few years ago a language inspectorate was set up in Estonia. "About fifteen professions were selected that could only be practiced with knowledge of Estonian," says Aet. "If you don't know Estonian, you can't be a doctor, a cab driver, or a salesperson—at least not in a state-owned store. You can't work in the state administration or at a school."

If the inspectorate catches a person who doesn't know Estonian, it issues a fine and a warning. The second time the fine is higher. The third time the culprit loses the right to practice the profession.

According to Mikhail Bogrym from Kohtla-Järve: "My wife is a teacher. We've spent a fortune on Estonian courses. They've fired doctors, including eminent specialists, because they didn't know Estonian well enough. But that's discrimination!"

However, so far nobody has had the courage to inspect Narva. As Aet says: "It's even impossible to buy milk in Estonian. Sometimes it really annoys me. Why do we fight so hard for our language? Because there are only a million of us. Though I do sometimes take advantage of the fact that I live in Narva."

"How?"

"I tend to break the speed limit. In Estonia the speeding fines are high. But whenever a policeman catches me, I talk very fast in Estonian. In Narva nobody knows it fluently. So I put on a grand show of indignation. I've never yet paid a fine here."

Mom, Dad, and the exam to be an Estonian

While Sasha was looking for TNT, I was having another cup of tea with Asya Mikhalichenko. We were sitting in a bar in Jõhvi, thirty miles from Narva.

The bar's customers are divided in two. Half of them have distinctly Estonian features. The other half have puffy Slavonic faces. Half are dressed modestly. The other half are in expensive brand-name tracksuits, with gold teeth and jewelry.

Asya speaks in Russian with her mom and her friends from Jõhvi, and in Estonian with the people she meets at college in Tartu.

What bothers her the most is that many Estonians judge her

by her family name. Because it's a Russian one, they don't want to be friends with her. "One time a boy came up to me. I'd never seen him in my life before. All he said was that he hated Russians, and then he just walked off."

Asya would prefer not to go to modern history classes. According to the students and lecturers, the USSR was responsible for all the evil in the world, and now it's Russia that's to blame. They stare at Asya as if she personally had invaded Estonia. And then she wishes the ground would open and swallow her up. "I'm not even 100 percent Russian," she complains.

Her mom is a Tatar, who moved to Estonia from Rostov-on-Don, immediately after graduating. She came out of love— her fiancé had been sent here to take up a job at a mine. In those days more than half the residents here made their living from oil shale extraction. The slag heaps start a few dozen yards from the city center.

Asya's mom was an inspector, checking the state of grocery stores. They had a great life. Estonia was the richest of all the Soviet republics. Anyone who could live here wanted to. In his book entitled *Estonia*, Jan Lewandowski cites an anecdote: upon arrival in Tallinn, the fencing team from the Karakalpak Autonomous Soviet Socialist Republic thought they were already in the West and asked for political asylum.

At Asya's home they wanted for nothing. The store managers used to bombard them with baskets of foodstuffs. Her father was a miner—the most prestigious job in the district. They didn't know a word of Estonian. But how could they, when all their neighbors were Russians?

When Asya reached the age of five, her father became a foreman. That was the first and only time her grandparents came to visit them—from Rostov it was a three-day journey by train.

A year later the Soviet Union collapsed, and everything began to go wrong. The new government refused to give her parents citizenship. They had to pass an "exam to be an Estonian." Her mom made six attempts at it. An Estonian neighbor saw a set of example questions. She didn't know half the answers, although she had spoken Estonian from birth.

So Asya's mom took some courses. She paid several hundred euros and studied into the small hours, but it was no use. Meanwhile the law changed, and without knowing Estonian she could no longer be a store inspector. She was fired. The store managers pretended not to know her. Finally, one of them took pity and gave her a job as a cleaner.

Her father had a tough time of it too. In the past all the shale oil had been sold to the USSR, but after 1991 there was nobody to buy it. One fine day her father lost his job. He couldn't find a new one and spent part of his time drinking and part of it watching TV. More and more often he just stared mindlessly out of the window.

About a year later, he went away to Russia. He said he'd be back once he'd pulled himself together. He hasn't been in touch for the past twelve years.

The lady president and the helpless prisoners

"Here the Russians are associated with nothing but loud music, fur coats, and dreadful makeup. But we Estonian Russians are nothing like the ones in Russia," says Vladislava Vashkina, a therapist and president of the Estonian Multiple Sclerosis Society.

Russian integration has been Estonia's biggest problem from the start. In 2005 a team of researchers based in Tallinn summarized its effects. The results were shocking. Well over half the

Estonians do not approve of the way Russians behave. One in three does not wish to work with them. Eighty-five percent of Estonians have no Russians among their closest friends. All these indicators are rising.

Other research tells us that from 1991 the number of suicides among Estonian Russians rose by 40 percent. And in Kohtla-Järve, by more than 50 percent.

I'm having my cup of tea with Mrs. Vashkina at the house of an Estonian woman called Ruth Tera, who runs a center for former prisoners and homeless people. The center is in a Stalinovka—a building dating from the 1950s. They're longer lasting than the later Khrushchovka buildings made of prefabricated concrete slabs. Even so, the plaster is crumbling off the center's building, and it could well collapse—the mining area starts two hundred yards from here.

"Kohtla-Järve is an extraordinary place," says Vladislava. "Twenty thousand people have Estonian citizenship, five thousand have Russian. And twenty thousand have no citizenship at all!"

"What do you mean, no citizenship?"

"They either haven't passed the exam to be an Estonian, or they haven't taken it. But they didn't want to become Russians."

"So how do they get by?"

"Normally. But they can't vote. And they need a visa to go to any other country, even Russia. Worse is what's happening in the minds of these stateless people. A few years ago we did some research on their sense of identity. The results were horrifying: they don't know where they belong. Estonia, where they were born, doesn't want them. And they're not at home in Russia either. It's a shock!"

"Why?"

"In the Soviet era, the Russians were privileged here. Suddenly, that was all over. They lost their prestige, their jobs, and their citizenship. Too much in just a few months. Many of them couldn't cope."

"On top of that, five of the mines were closed down in a short period of time—Kohtla, Sompa, Tammiku, Ahtme, and Kiviõli," adds Ruth. "People weren't ready for that. They had to be helped."

Her center was designed to be a place for former prisoners with nowhere to go following their release.

"In the mid-1990s a large number of people who had gone behind bars in the Soviet era were released," says Ruth. "Their families had left for Russia, and they had no one here. They were in a state of shock—a different country, different money, stores, goods, and rights. Russia wouldn't give them citizenship because they were criminals. Nor would Estonia, because they didn't know the language. And for anyone over fifty it's really hard to learn a language. Estonian is in the Finno-Ugric group of languages. It has fourteen tenses."

In the mid-1990s unemployment reached its peak too.

"Luckily, that has changed now," says Vladislava. "There are courses for former miners, to teach them to become construction workers, welders, or pastry chefs. Lots of them have found work."

The expensive chandeliers and the professor's birthday

"If the Russians think they've got it bad here, let them go to Russia," says Mart Pechter, who is 100 percent Estonian.

We're sitting at the Moskva bar, a favorite venue for Tallinn's social elite. There are expensive chandeliers hanging from the ceiling, waitresses in short skirts, and cut-glass mirrors on the walls. Lots of glitter and pizzazz.

Mart is a student of political sciences. Like 85 percent of Estonians, he hasn't a single Russian in his circle of friends. And he doesn't want any, even though half the residents of his city are Russians. "I have a Russian neighbor. Sometimes I say hello to him in Estonian—it's *tere*. But he pretends he can't understand me. Goddammit, we're living in independent Estonia. Let's talk in Estonian!"

The Bronze Soldier? Mart used to pass it every day on his way to the university. Once a year he saw a handful of gold-toothed old boys jangling their medals and some women with bunches of daisies. They used to meet there on May 9, their Victory Day. It would never have occurred to Mart to ban these defenseless representatives of the past from celebrating their anniversaries. He regarded their traditions as folklore.

Everything changed a year ago. "Some right-wing troublemakers tried to protest against the veterans. The police nabbed them. No big deal, but the message that went out in the media was: Estonian cops arrest Estonian youth so that the invaders can lay some flowers."

"And, so what?"

"I agree that it shouldn't be like that. My own memory of the USSR is very faint. Just the May Day parades—I loved them. Tallinn was sad and gray, but the parades were bright and colorful. I also remember the Baltic chain. Two million people from Lithuania, Latvia, and Estonia stood in line and held hands. It was a peace demonstration over a distance of 370 miles. They sang songs, and it was fabulous. Great fun for the kids. Even the Russians joined in with us. They knew the USSR was total shit too. And I remember my father cursing his Russian boss. He worked at an academic institute. From the associate professors up, almost all of them were Russian. They had an easy life here. My father once went to see the boss, Professor Antonov, to ask about his prospects for promotion. And the professor said: 'Comrade, I never see you at the club. You weren't at my birthday party. I hardly know you! How can I know if you deserve promotion?' My friend says it might be a difference in temperaments. Because the Russians like to party, to fraternize, and clap each other on the back. That's what matters to them.

"Estonians are cold. Even after a lot of vodka, we don't open up. Telling someone about your problems isn't part of our mind-set.

"But now my father says he would have left the Bronze Soldier there. Because it's an idealized soldier, not an invader. The invaders and the upstarts came after it."

"What about you? What do you think?"

"I think the Russians need to be taken down a peg. One in four of them doesn't speak Estonian. Not a word. That's no good! Anyone can learn a few sentences. They behave as if they're a great superpower. Learning Estonian is beneath their dignity. Sometimes they need to be reminded that this isn't Russia anymore."

"They haven't forgotten—half of them haven't got passports."

"Why should they have them? They haven't learned the language, because they thought Russia would be coming back here. They didn't believe the USSR really had collapsed. And now they know that Russia will always support them. If it weren't for Big Brother across the border, we'd have come to terms with them long ago."

The two miners and the drunken brothers

The young people in Kohtla-Järve have a choice in the evenings between the Alex bar or a park surrounded by Stalinovkas. They prefer the park—here, they don't have to pay for anything.

They like to sit on the benches behind the statue of two miners proudly wielding heavy pickaxes. The residents call these figures "the teetotalers." From one year to the next, from the height of their abstinence they watched every May Day parade go by. On each national holiday since 1991, the Estonian flag has fluttered next to them. I open my conversation with the local high school students by asking them about this flag.

"I associate it with my parents' persecution," says Julia. "My dad was a brilliant surgeon. He graduated from the medical academy in Leningrad. He never learned the Estonian language, so they fired him. They disregarded the fact that all his patients were Russians. These days he's a driving instructor."

"It's my country's flag," says Sasha. "The fact that this country doesn't always treat me fairly is another matter."

"The Estonians are fascists," says Ivan. "But it's our country too. We should civilize them."

"Fascists?" I ask, trying to understand.

"Yes," says Ivan. "They never fought against fascism. They didn't support the Red Army."

"Because they didn't want to be annexed by the land of Soviets."

"Because they're fascists. Each year they hold an SS veterans' rally here."

Ivan is the most radical. He was the only one who attended the riots in Tallinn. The rest had other problems besides the Bronze Soldier.

"A month ago I got my Estonian passport," says Misha. "Lately, the exams have become easier. During the holidays, I'm going to see my cousin in London. I'll earn a bit of money."

"I don't have a passport," says Nastya. "I haven't yet decided which sort to get. I have lots of family in Russia. But I'm drawn to the West too. Though I think I'll apply for the Russian one. I want to be an actor, and the best drama school is in Moscow."

"I don't have a passport either," says Veronika. "I'm waiting for my mom to get one. I don't want to have different citizenship from her. I was born in independent Estonia, and I could have had a passport at once. But I'm waiting. It's a sort of civic protest."

I ask the students if they feel more Russian or European. Only Sasha feels more of a Russian.

"My aunts, uncles, grandma, and grandpa are all Russians," he says. "The fact that my parents are here has to do with where their work happened to send them, rather than choice. When they retire, they want to go back to Russia."

Barely 10 percent of the Russians here give the same sort of answer as Sasha. According to research done in 2005, almost 70 percent identify with independent Estonia, even though only half of them have Estonian citizenship.

"Even if I get a Russian passport, I'll feel like a European," says Nastya. "We're very different from our relatives in Russia. They're not terribly fond of us. They envy us our Estonian prosperity. My grandma calls me 'my little Estonian.'"

"When I visited my cousins outside Moscow, I realized I was nothing like them," says Misha. "For me, the Internet, chat rooms and Skype are obvious. They're the same age as me, but they don't even know what all that is, whether you carry it in a bucket or a spoon."

"My father's brothers came to see him from the other side of the Urals," says Julia. "They had a few drinks; then the vodka ran out, so they picked up the keys and headed for the car. My father lay down in the doorway and said, 'Over my dead body! You'll kill someone!' In Estonia drunk driving is a very serious offense. My uncles looked at my dad and said, 'You're not a Russki anymore. You're not our brother anymore.'"

TNT and Hugo Boss clothing

Asya Mikhalichenko's mom signed up for yet another Estonian course. The seventh time, she managed to pass the exam. If it all goes well, six months from now she'll be an Estonian.

The government in Tallinn is giving serious thought to starting up a Russian-language TV channel.

There are some Estonian Internet sites where you can still find Hugo Boss clothing at bargain prices.

My friend Jaan has calmed down now. He thinks the outburst of emotion did everyone some good. It will have made the Russians aware that, in spite of all, it's better to live in Estonia than on the Neva. And the Estonians will have realized they do too little to make the Russians feel at home in Estonia, and that it's only badly treated Russians who might form a fifth column.

Before finding the TNT, Sasha called Vladislava Vashkina. He used to go to her for therapy, and for him she's an authority. He asked her what to do. "Keep well away from it," said Vladislava. It worked. For now, both the station and the airport in Tallinn are intact.

VI. Hibernation

And the fact that they're hibernating means our bears are making progress on the road to freedom. They're no longer living from one day to the next. They've learned to prepare for tougher times.

Poland: Hobbits at the State Farm

▲▲ t's poverty and unemployment that have brought us out of our houses," says Gandalf. "Otherwise no one would make such a fool of himself." I met him in person at a former PGR—or State Agricultural Farm—near Koszalin in Poland.

I'm in the Lublin area with a small group of people—each of whom occupies the post of *sołtys*, or local community leader—on a tour of villages that have found their feet in the twenty-first century. We've already been to places known as World's End, Labyrinths, Fairy Tales, Bicycles, and the Healthy Living Hamlet. The community leaders are looking to see if something similar could be set up in their own villages.

The next stop is Sierakowo Sławieńskie—otherwise known as the Hobbits' Village. "As long as none of them bites me," jokes one of the community leaders.

We park the bus by some wooden cottages inhabited by characters out of Tolkien. The main attraction is a game in the woods, where you can meet them in person. In June alone, three thousand visitors showed up at the Hobbits' Village.

We buy tickets for fifteen zlotys each (under five dollars), including a bowl of soup and a sausage. Gandalf himself supplies us with maps. We set off for the woods.

Gandalf hasn't time to watch TV

"Eight years ago Wacław Idziak, the expert from Koszalin, came here. 'I can see a Hobbits' Village here,' he said. 'What are hobbits?' we asked.

"Getting started was tough. The old crones outside the store would say, 'They paint their silly faces and traipse about the village. Shame on them!' To which I'd reply, 'Once a month the mailman knocks on your door and hands you your pension. But he only brings me bills. Why should I feel ashamed of wanting to earn a living?'"

The woman who plays Gandalf has fair hair and is in her late thirties. She's the one in charge in the village square when groups of children go into the woods.

"The children sometimes say Gandalf wasn't a woman. I reply curtly, 'How do you know? Have you ever examined him?' That does the trick. Of course, I only say that to the older ones. I tell the younger ones to pull on my beard. Or else I scare them.

"Sometimes they tug my beard and ask why I've got a floor mop on my face. Or they say, 'You're dressed up.' To which I say, 'You're dressed too.' I'm not going to be pushed around. I've been through too much in life.

"Things are better now. And there's work at last. I'm Gandalf until three in the afternoon. Then I change my clothes and

I'm Małgorzata again. I jump in the car with the other girls, and we're off to our other jobs.

"Sierakowo? My husband was sent here by the forestry commission. The first time I came here, twenty years ago, it was July, and the broom was in flower everywhere. It was all lovely and yellow. I thought we were coming to live in paradise. But in November, when we finally moved, it was cold, gray, and dismal. There was nothing left of the broom but stumps. It was enough to make you cry.

"For years and years, I sat on my butt at home. I was a fairly typical housewife, washing, cleaning, and cooking. And taking my child to the hospital. My daughter had trouble with her liver and spleen. Three times a week I had to take her to Koszalin on the bus.

"Thanks to the hobbits, the village has changed. And I've changed too. I used to spend all my free time sitting in front of the TV. I knew all the programs by heart. Now I can't remember when I last watched TV—I think it was in May.

"Everyone used to ask, 'Where is Sierakowo?' I'd reply, 'Sianów district, the place where they make matches. Now when I say Sierakowo, everyone says: 'The hobbits!'

"After four years, I went on the trail through the woods for the first time for myself. As soon as I saw the trolls, I took to my heels. I ran all the way to the surfaced road before I said to myself, 'You idiot, what are you running away for? Those trolls are your colleagues!'"

Dr. Idziak from the top of the ladder

After a few hundred yards on a surfaced road you're at the end of the village. There's a slight rise here, from which you can see almost the entire village spread out before you: a little church, a few dozen houses that were originally German, and a school, which any day now will stop being a school.

Wacław Idziak, promoter of themed villages, found this place while working on a strategy for the Sianów district. "The residents helped me to make maps of their areas. We were looking for attractive places. The map of Sierakowo was incredible: megalithic tombs in the woods and some stone circles. Tolkien sprang to mind immediately."

After studying Polish philology at Poznań University, he worked at a cultural center, then lectured in sociology and philosophy. In 1989 he wanted to be as close as he could to the transformation, so he resigned from the college and took a job at a bakery. "I created new kinds of bread. Then I ran a wholesaler's, selling organic foods, until I became manager of the Regional Development Agency in Koszalin. By then I was already trying to promote themed villages. But people had other things on their minds. And from the top of the ladder, it was hard to do anything at the bottom. So I resigned from the agency, and my wife and I went into the field.

"Our first attempts? They were at a place called Wierzbinek. We taught people how to find cultural references. *Wierzba* means a willow—Goethe wrote about willows, and they have associations with devils and Chopin.

"People sometimes think we only care about money, and that we want to make a fast buck out of the hobbits for ourselves. Not true. We have money from EU grants. We've had assistance from lots of charitable foundations. I received a grant from Ashoka, an organization that supports social entrepreneurs. I haven't had a penny from the hobbits.

"How did it all start? We were known around here. We'd organized fetes in the local villages, events with jugglers, and arts workshops. The people from Sierakowo knew about all that. But the first time I told them about the hobbits, I thought one of them would stand up and tap himself on the forehead."

The Witch with the Internet

"Some of them have tapped their foreheads. But how can you help it around here? I, for instance, give the children a drink that's made from a handful of spiders, a handful of mosquitoes, and bog water," says the Witch.

On the sign leading to her kingdom, it says: "The firehouse-and-clubroom at Sierakowo Sławieńskie was built using the PZU's preventative fund, with contributions from the public." (The PZU is Poland's leading insurance company.) Behind the door there's a small library with an Internet connection. This is where the Witch changes into Edyta, a woman with cropped fair hair and a very friendly smile.

"How did I get involved with the hobbits? One time my cousin couldn't go and be the Witch, so I said, 'I'll go for you, but what do I have to say?' So I put on a sack, painted my face black, and went off to scare the children."

Her cousin is an Ent. We're sitting together around the table in the clubroom. "I've been involved from the start of the project. Because it was all organized around the school. And under my real name, Bogusława, I work at the school. That's to say, I used to. Because the local authority has just closed our school.

"We've known for ages it was closing down. I was supposed to get my diploma in 2004. But I was scared I'd be too expensive a teacher and nobody would take me on. A teacher with a diploma has to be paid more—that's the law. So I chose to remain cheaper.

"Only this year did I finally change my mind. I've now done some postgraduate studies, and I'm taking more courses. What must be will be. And it has paid off. I'm going to work at the clubroom in Sianów.

"It's a real shame for us to lose the school. This year our children won the district nativity-play contest. We had a computer room with new equipment. For Bilbo's birthday, we put on a puppet play. There are plenty of cities where there's less going on than at our little school.

"But there were only twelve children. The local authority calculated that it cost three hundred thousand zlotys (then about eighty-five thousand dollars) a year. We lost by one vote."

The lady sołtys is shelling peas

Apparently the lady *sołtys*—the community leader—is on the warpath against the hobbits. Why? No one's entirely sure. At first she was involved. The local mayor bought her an ostrich, and she was going to show it to the children as an attraction.

But then things took a turn. She started locking her gate and keeping the ostrich out of sight. Then it died. What was it all about? No one knows. I'm going to ask.

The *sołtys* is called Mariola, and she's no-nonsense, down-to-earth, energetic, and busy. She and her sons have just been picking peas, and they have to be shelled. She doesn't want to talk about the hobbits. "You can write that I wish them well," she says, and tries to say good-bye. I can't allow that. Nobody knows as much about the life of a village as the *sołtys*. So we agree that I'll help with the shelling, and meanwhile we'll have a chat about the village and its problems.

"But not a word about the hobbits!" she stresses.

We sit down. I obediently start shelling. "The people here are mainly from Operation Vistula.* They're hardworking. There was never much hanging around outside the store with a bottle of wine.

"Problems? The main one is the road. It's full of holes. Lately there was a fire at the farmworkers' building—the firefighters had a very tough drive to get there. I won't even mention the ambulance. Most of our people are old. They're afraid that if anything happens to them, the ambulance won't get here in time.

"A second problem is the poor phone signal. Hardly any cell phones work well here. In the twenty-first century, right near the German border. Unthinkable.

"The third is that there are fewer and fewer young people here. Fifty of the two hundred villagers were born before or during the war. The young people run off to wherever they can."

Gollum smokes Marlboros

Gollum, also known as Zenon Pusz, runs the village store. We're sitting on a small bench, drinking Tyskie beer and smoking Marlboros. We're remembering the days when in the countryside you smoked filterless cigarettes and drank cheap wine known as "brainfuck."

That's ancient history now. Hardly anyone buys cheap wine at Gollum's store. His regular customers are sitting at a small

---

* Operation Vistula was the forced resettlement, carried out in 1947, of some Ukrainian ethnic minorities from southeastern Poland to the so-called Recovered Territories in the west of the country, which had belonged to Germany before the Second World War.

table next to us, downing beer and talking about how democracy is falling apart in Poland.

"Imagine taking away your driver's license just for riding a bike . . . Even in Gomułka's day they never did that . . ."

"'Cause you were riding that bike when you were wasted, Jaś," observes a man who's not as inebriated.

"It's all the same. In the old days you could even drive a tractor while under the influence. You could always come to terms with the old militia. It's a police state now."

Let's get back to the hobbits. "Gollum? He used to be one of them, but he went crazy. Because of the ring. He killed his brother for the ring," Zenon starts to say, but some more customers appear, and he has to go behind the counter to serve them.

"There was a similar story in the next village," recalls the cycling enthusiast. "But it wasn't a ring they quarreled over—it was a girl."

"Nooo, it was a piece of land," the other one reminds him. "One brother killed the other. Gospel truth."

Zenon comes back to his half-smoked cigarette and his interrupted story. "When a tour group comes I say: 'Greetings to you, hobbits. I'm a hobbit too.' Then they shout: 'No you're not!' And they go look for the ring in the pond."

"Tell him how you made the pond, Zenon!"

"By accident. A few years ago I planted some potatoes. The stream flooded and the potatoes went to rot. But I dragged the cultivator over that patch and dug out a small pit. That's where they look for the ring. It's only knee deep, but I tell them it's ten feet.

"Last year, one woman clung to the rope with her hands and feet, though her butt was already touching the bottom. She was terrified."

"Hey, Zenon, perhaps you could fix me up with a job?" says the cyclist.

"Would you rather be a troll or a dwarf?" asks Gollum, laughing. "You see, our parents lived entirely off the land. But now we hardly cultivate it at all. Last year I converted twelve acres into forest. The EU gives us money. If the local authority gives permission, all the land here will be converted into forest."

The Elf Queen likes the movie

"Something's wrong with the kids these days," says Queen Galadriel, sharing her thoughts. "Rather than pick flowers for me, the Elf Queen, their first thought is to look for sticks to fight off the trolls. We were more peaceful than that."

This year the queen—a.k.a. Małgorzata—plucked up the courage to take a job at Espersen, a fish-processing firm.

"Why do I say 'I plucked up the courage'? Because if you haven't worked for a long time, it's hard to make that first effort. But seriously, it's the first time I've had a job."

On the website we read that Espersen's international mission is to supply Baltic Sea fish to quality-conscious customers in Europe and the USA; their standard products include frozen fish blocks, frozen fillets, special cuts, and a range of breaded fish.

These standard products are deboned and packed by the Elf Queen. Right now she's on a month's leave. She's not sure what's going to happen next.

"I might have to resign from the hobbits. That would be a pity. But the hobbits don't provide a pension, Espersen does.

"The kids? I'm a good character. From me, they get an artifact that's supposed to protect them."

"What do they get?"

"Like I said, an artifact. But if the group can't answer my question, I keep a hostage. What sort of thing do I ask? About the characters in Tolkien. Or a riddle: 'Yellow and red, they fall from the trees, they're carried about by the wind and the breeze. What are they?'

"I get the riddles from the Internet. It's hard to imagine life in the village without a computer now.

"Last year we had a very large number of tourists. I think everyone's happy about it. Just a small village, and so many tour buses.

"When they see me, sometimes they shout, 'Red Riding Hood!' And then I say, 'Sorry, friends, but that's a different story.'

"Though sometimes you get a child who's read Tolkien and doesn't like it here, saying it's not like the book. I haven't read the book, but we did go and see the movie. You've got to like reading. I don't. But I really enjoyed the movie."

The First Troll is waiting for the local authority

"If I raise my wrist, I can't move my fingers," says the First Troll, showing me a hand that was badly mangled in an accident at the PGR (the state farm). "My hand was dragged between two metal rollers. The doctors only managed to save one tendon.

"But my attitude to life is that you only live once and there's no point worrying. If things are bad today, maybe tomorrow will be better. Just like now. In April my home burned down. We were living in the old farmworkers' building. The local authority says they'll rebuild it by November, but they haven't even started. I'm living at the school, with my wife and kids. So what am I to do, weep?

"Why Sierakowo? My father had an accident, and at the age of fourteen I had to run his farm myself. Later I ended up at the animal-breeding PGR at Sowno. And I found myself a wife there. She wanted to stay at the PGR, because they gave you everything there. When the PGR collapsed, we went on welfare.

"The hobbits? What I like best about it is that all the money stays in the village. If there's a fete, our ladies do the cooking, our storekeeper sells the beer, and our teacher plays the music. Our own people get to earn something, not outsiders.

"I find it easy to communicate with the kids."

"How could he fail to, when he's made eleven of his own?" says the blacksmith of Middle-earth, a.k.a. Stefan, from behind his newspaper.

"I've only got seven!" says the First Troll indignantly. The blacksmith refuses to back off. "Come on! Every other redhead who comes on the tour is yours."

The Troll dismissively waves a hand—the intact one.

"We had training courses too. They told us to approach the children the same way as they approach you. If the kid's nice, be nice too. If he shouts, so do you.

"I've done thirty or forty courses in all. Never in my life did I expect to do so much more learning after trade school. And we travel the world! I've been to Austria, the Czech Republic, and Slovakia. And England too.

"But we also teach them about nature. The city kids don't know what a duck looks like. And if the Witch tells them to go catch some mosquitoes, they're off to look for them. They've no idea mosquitoes don't fly around in the daytime."

The Second Troll is counting on the hobbits

"The worst thing is not knowing what we've got for certain. If the local community lets us have the former school building, we can go ahead with some major development plans."

The Second Troll—a.k.a. Józef—is the manager of Hobbits' Village. "About thirty people earn a living from the hobbits now. We receive several thousand visitors. We're professionals. There's some real money starting to come in. How much? Hard to calculate. But in the season it adds up to several thousand zlotys per person.

"But if they don't give us the school, it's hard to say if we'll be able to keep going. And it'd be a pity for all this to go to waste. The people have changed. Some of them were afraid to say a word to anyone. These days they're outgoing and talkative."

He used to work as a shipfitter. Then he went his own way. "At first it didn't go badly. My brother and I had five stores in the local villages. We took out a lease on a vehicle. But society began to get poorer. Who's come worst out of it? My pals! You can't give your pals credit? Yes, you can, but unfortunately we've got nothing but pals around here. So at just one store we were owed seven thousand in credit. We were the boldest, and thus among those who took the worst beating in those years. Now we're the boldest too. People come here from all over the country to learn from us.

"You see that shed? I built it a dozen years ago. My friends and I were going to make parts for the little Fiats, but it didn't work out. Now it's going to be the Troll's Inn. We've just set up a company. We're going to try to live off nothing but the hobbits."

"Is it going to work?"

"Oh yes, it'll be great. And if not, we'll do something else."

Dr. Idziak does some juggling

It's the end of the tour. Wacław Idziak is standing opposite the group of community leaders from the Lublin area. He's holding four little balls. With his right hand, he keeps throwing one of them in the air and catching it, slowly and steadily. "For years on end it was like this in the village. You only had to master a single skill: sowing the fields, raising stock, whatever. But now times have changed." And he starts to juggle. "Nowadays you have to try to do this," he says, juggling three balls at once. "Or this." And he tosses up two balls, then just one by turns.

The Lublin area community leaders shake their heads. "It'll never catch on at our place."

"That's what they said here too," replies Idziak.

The community leaders shake their heads again. "There's poverty around here. Where we live it's not quite so bad that we have to make hobbits of ourselves."

VII. Lions to Africa

*My main rule for these trips is this: act dumber
than you really are. Best of all, much dumber.*

Serbia: Pop Art Radovan

▲▲ Ladies and gentlemen, this is where Mr. Karadžić lived.
These people are his neighbors. Better not take pictures,
sir. They're fed up with journalists. You see—they're shouting.
Please don't shout! It's just a tour group. Two Poles, two Russians, and a Japanese. Please don't be concerned. This is just an
unfortunate incident. We Serbs are usually very friendly. Oh
look, that lady with the dog is smiling."

It's August 3, 2008. I'm in Belgrade on a walking tour in the
footsteps of Radovan Karadžić, who hid here while disguised as
an expert in alternative medicine, Dr. Dragan Dabić. We're visiting his apartment block, his local store, and his favorite bar.
The tour is called Pop Art Radovan.

The tour guide is a girl of about twenty. When Karadžić was
laying siege to Sarajevo, she was barely knee high. Whatever happens, she never stops smiling. "Did you notice? There's something in his mailbox. No, better not go over there, sir. I know you
people from Japan always take a lot of pictures, but this time it's
not such a good idea."

We're gazing at the most ordinary apartment block in the world. The same old sun is blazing away like hell. The same old geraniums are blooming in a flowerpot, just as he saw them every time he came outside.

There's no mountain hideout, no pistols, and no shoot-out. There's a children's climbing frame and seven benches painted green. It's a six-story block on which someone has now spray-painted: "Radovan Karadžić Street."

On July 22, 2008, he left this house carrying several bags. He walked a few hundred yards, to the number 73 bus stop. According to some, he was going on vacation. Others say he'd realized that the new government would do all it could to send him to the Hague. He boarded the bus, and within a quarter of an hour he was caught. The Butcher of Bosnia.

One thousand years in jail

Where did the name Dragan Dabić come from? Apparently the real Dabić was an engineer in Sarajevo before the war. But can we be sure of that? Nothing about this whole business is entirely certain. The Western journalists in Belgrade say the police are deliberately taking us for a ride. And the authorities are counting on us to seek out the owner of his identity card, by running off to local supermarkets to ask which was his favorite cheese, and to the medical clinics to inquire about the healing methods he used. They're doing everything they can to sidetrack us on to nonessential questions about the details of Dr. Dabić's life.

All in an effort to stop us from asking the most important things: how is it possible that the worst criminal since the Second World War was calmly walking around downtown Belgrade?

"But the details matter too," stresses one of the foreign journalists. "To understand today's Serbia, you have to understand the double life of the good Doctor Dabić and the bad Mister Karadžić."

So let's seek out the owner of the identity card. The most probable version goes like this: Dragan Dabić lived in Sarajevo. He was killed by a bullet from a Serbian sniper in the spring of 1993 while running down the street to the square where humanitarian aid was due to be distributed.

By then, Sarajevo had been under siege for months on end by the troops of Radovan Karadžić, president of the Republika Srpska (Serbian Republic), which is now part of Bosnia.

Life in the city was getting tougher and tougher. There was no water, food, or bandages.

The story of the first death of Dragan Dabić was told on national television by his brother, Mladen, who lives in Sarajevo to this day. "The bullet was fired from the Vraca district. Karadžić's troops had outposts there. My brother, a Serb, was killed by Serbian soldiers. When I found out later on that Karadžić was pretending to be him, I was horrified. How could anyone be so cynical?"

Almost four years under siege cost Sarajevo more than twelve thousand victims. Fifteen hundred of them were children.

At the Hague Tribunal, Karadžić faced up to a thousand years in jail. The most serious charge against him was genocide. In 1995 his soldiers had carried out the mass murder of the Muslim civilian population of a town called Srebrenica.

"The women and children were told to go to the right, the men to the left. Whether a boy was still a child or already a man was decided by a piece of string that was hung at a height of five feet. . . . Any boy who was taller than that was taken away from his mother," writes Wojciech Tochman about Srebrenica in his book *Like Eating a Stone*. "The following spring the women found out from the radio that teams from the Hague Tribunal were working around Srebrenica. Thirty-five hundred bodies had been found beneath the freshly disturbed earth."*

"The youngest person to survive the scores of executions . . . was only seventeen years old. As he was being taken out of the truck with a group of men, blindfolded and hands bound, they all asked for a sip of water. 'I didn't want to die thirsty,' he said years later," wrote Bosnian journalist Emir Suljagić in his book, *Postcards from the Grave*.† Suljagić was one of the few who survived the Serbian army attack on Srebrenica.

Dražen Erdemović was forced by his commanders to execute the Muslims from Srebrenica. "The boy was not blindfolded and Dražen saw his face, though he had promised himself that he would not look at the prisoners' faces, as it made shooting more difficult. The boy might have been fifteen, perhaps younger. . . . When the prisoners knelt down in front of the squad, just before the command to shoot came, Dražen heard the boy's voice. Mother, he whispered. Mother! . . . A minute later the boy was dead." So Slavenka Drakulić re-creates one day in the life of Dražen in her book *They Would Never Hurt a Fly*.‡

Almost eight thousand men and boys were killed at Srebrenica. The youngest was fourteen.

---

* Wojciech Tochman, *Like Eating a Stone*, translated by Antonia Lloyd-Jones (New York: Atlas, 2008).

† Emir Suljagić, *Postcards from the Grave*, translated by Lejla Haverić (London: Saqi, 2005).

‡ Slavenka Drakulić, *They Would Never Hurt a Fly* (London: Abacus, 2004).

Dabić's second death

Dragan Dabić died for the second time at the Serbian state prosecution building. This time it just took a few snips with a pair of scissors for the long-haired, charismatic expert in alternative medicine to be gone for good.

Yet some people say that Karadžić had documents in the name of a different Dabić—a small-scale farmer from a village called Ruma, some forty miles from Belgrade. Apparently, the identity card that Karadžić used was a copy of one belonging to Dabić the farmer who, as the Western journalists confirm, lives without a computer or a cell phone. "I never asked for all this fame," said Dabić, the farmer, on BBC television, which he had no idea existed until now.

Where did Karadžić get Dragan Dabić's documents? It's a mystery. Several sets of documents in various names were found at his apartment.

I wanted to feel the current

Nowadays it's hard to track down any of Karadžić-Dabić's patients. When you do find them, they talk about their visits to him with some embarrassment. First, because it probably feels odd to discover that your doctor has turned out to be somebody completely different. Second, because alternative medicine has been ridiculed here for some years as pure superstition.

Third, because Dragan Dabić often treated intimate conditions, such as impotence and infertility.

Yelena S., age thirty, is a friend of my contacts in Belgrade. She's slender, well groomed, and down-to-earth: "The treatment?

A friend persuaded me to go for it. She'd been to a meeting where Dabić talked about diet. She said he was from the States, but he'd been living in India and China. He was meant to charge five hundred dinars (then about nine dollars) for a consultation, but usually he took nothing. He gave the impression that money had no value for him.

"At the time I had problems with my kidneys and was at risk of dialysis. I was trying to find help everywhere and anywhere.

"First, he looked deep into my eyes. Then he checked my pulse and told me to stick out my tongue. Finally, he placed his hands on my back. He held them there; then after a while he let go and shook them. After that I had a warm feeling. To finish he made me a sort of amulet. I never wore it—I was going to throw it away. But now I'm sure I'll keep it as a souvenir.

"I didn't have much confidence in him. He looked like a charlatan. He had long hair tied in a ponytail and a beard like Santa Claus. At one point he told me that cosmic energy came to him via the hair and beard. I thought I'd fall off the chair.

"Though my kidneys have gotten stronger. But I don't know if it's thanks to him, because I tried a lot of things, including prayer and fasting."

Dušan M. is a regular at a bar called the Madhouse, which was Dabić's favorite hangout. He's an ardent patriot, with a slight squint and very short shorts. "I once complained to Karadžić—that's to say, Dabić—that I was going to have an operation on my leg. It had healed crooked after a motorbike accident.

"My mother told me to go see him because at her village in Montenegro there was a local quack of the same kind. She said, 'If he can't help you, no one can.'

"I knew Dabić—he quite often came in for a beer. He'd clap me on the back and ask after my health.

"I don't think anyone in our housing development was born in

Belgrade. They started building it in the late 1970s. They settled military personnel here with their families. My father was assigned an apartment because he was an officer in the Yugoslav army.

"Plenty of people moved here during the war—Serbian refugees from Bosnia-Herzegovina. Very good Serbs. Some of them had fought in the war. You could say that for Mr. Karadžić it was the ideal place to live.

"My leg? I did go to him. 'Dr. Dabić,' I said, 'can you help with badly healed bones? They're going to rebreak it. Can't anything be done?'

"He took a look at me from behind his thick glasses. He said he'd had some wine, and he couldn't do any healing after alcohol. He told me to come to his apartment the next day.

"It was very clean in the apartment. There were two rooms—in one of them he slept and worked at a large computer. I wondered at the time why he needed such a big computer. Later on I read that he'd been gathering documents for his defense at the Hague.

"Next to the computer was a photo of four boys in American basketball uniforms. Dr. Dabić said they were his grandsons who live in the States.

"Treatment? He laid his hands on my legs. He asked if I could feel the current. I couldn't feel anything. But there was something about his tone of voice that made me want to feel it. So I said, 'Yes, I can.'

"Even so, they rebroke those bones at the hospital. But they say it has grown together well now. I don't know if that's true, because I'm still limping."

This is an apolitical tour

"Ladies and gentlemen, this is where Dr. Dabić did his shopping. Tomatoes, thirty-nine dinars. Pears, sixty-nine dinars.* They say he fed himself a very costly diet. Nothing but fruit and vegetables. And cheese. Apparently, he was adamant that everything he ate should be from Serbia. The saleswoman says she also has tomatoes from Spain on offer. They're bigger, nicer looking, and not much more expensive. But he always chose the Serbian ones.

"Now please look to your right—here's the bar, the Madhouse, where he used to sit under his own portrait, drinking Bear's Blood wine and chatting to people. Everyone was sure he was called Dragan Dabić and was a doctor of alternative medicine. The wine? Why don't you give it a try? Our agency will treat you. Don't you like it? It's cheap wine. Unsophisticated people drink it. Dr. Dabić lived a very simple life."

There's an awful mess at the Madhouse. The tables are wiped clean only when someone remembers to do it. Yelen beer is the most popular, but you can also get Montenegrin Nikšićko. There's plenty of everything—beer mugs, beer mats, dishcloths, and bottles. And in place of honor are the portraits. We ask the tour guide about them.

"The one on the right is General Mladić. They haven't caught him yet.† Apparently, he's hiding somewhere in the mountains, in an old bunker used by Marshal Tito. We do a tour in the footsteps of Tito too. And the NATO bombings. I'll show you our catalog.

---

* At the time, there were about fifty-five Serbian dinars to the US dollar.

† Mladić was arrested on May 26, 2011, after he was found hiding in a remote village. He was extradited to the Hague, where his trial began on May 16, 2012, and still continues.

"The one on the left? What do you mean, you don't know? Well, okay, you're from Japan. You've no reason to know. That's Slobodan Milošević, the former president. Hello, the gentleman from Poland—sorry, I didn't hear your question. Is what legal? Putting up these portraits? Why should it be illegal? This is a democracy. I guess you can put up whatever you like in Poland too. Oh no, you're trying to provoke me, but this is an apolitical tour. That's not nice. Please come and board the bus."

I miss Doctor Dabić

Dragan Dabić's friends are missing him. Mina Minić, a therapist who was Dabić's guru, tells me over the phone: "Please understand that it's not Karadžić I miss. I only ever knew him as Doctor Dabić—a very nice man, whose thoughts were taken up with astrology and levitation."

Dabić was going to write a book about Minić. Out of gratitude, Minić gave him a new first name—David. After the biblical king, because Minić and Dabić's ideology was closely connected with Christianity.

"Ours is an atheist version of Orthodoxy," says Minić. "We took all the best elements from the Orthodox Church: the mysticism, the meditation, the healing by fasting and prayer. Did you know that Orthodox monks were capable of levitating? That in the early Christian church it was a fairly universal ability? What happened to the monks? What keeps them to the ground? Those were the sort of questions we asked ourselves. And we rejected the institutional church—its tinsel, its pomp, and its involvement in politics.

"Now I've been reading that as president Karadžić was very

close to the church. Which means that the whole time he was deceiving me.

"Karadžić—I mean Dabić—fasted twice a week, on Fridays and Wednesdays. He sought analogies between Orthodoxy and the things he learned in India and China. Now I know that he never went there at all. But he talked about it very convincingly. I thought he was a great sage. But he was just a great actor," says Minić.

"He mainly listened," says Miško Kovijanić, owner of the Madhouse. "That's not typical for Serbia, where people mainly talk rather than listen.

"The people living here are poor, and wherever you find poverty, that's where they do the most gabbing about politics. Dabić used to sit under the portrait of Karadžić and watch us. We talked away many a winter evening like that. Occasionally, if someone went too far, Dr. Dabić would shake his head and say, 'It's not that simple, my children.' But never once did he say what his own views were.

"It's a pity he didn't tell us the truth. Nobody would have given him away—we'd have given him even better protection. Only decent Serbs come here."

"Meaning what?" I ask.

"Patriots. Former soldiers. Opponents of the goddamn European Union. But I understand why he couldn't tell us. He was very careful, but even so someone betrayed him. I read in the paper that five million dollars was paid for his head.

"Why the Madhouse? When we were building the bar eight years ago, my wife called. It was terribly noisy. 'I'll have to go outside,' I said: 'it's a madhouse in here.' The workers picked it up, and it stuck.

"But we've had a real madhouse here ever since they caught our Dr. Dabić. Journalists, tourists, everyone. The worst of all are the nationalists. I don't like to say it, I'm a Serb and I love Serbia. But they tried to set fire to my bar because I sell Coca-Cola—in other words, an American drink. Is that normal? I had to hide the entire refrigerator. Now they show up here every day.

"You know what? My dream is that one day the door will open and Dr. Dabić will walk in, cool as ice. I'll buy him a glass of wine and say, 'Doctor, what an adventure you've had!' And he'll sit down, nod his head, and tell us how they apologized to him at the Hague Tribunal for their mistake. I didn't know Karadžić personally; I only respect him as a leader. He wanted Serbia to be just for the Serbs, and that's how it should be.

"But I do miss Dabić. And the peace and quiet we had a few weeks ago."

I was not his lover

When I arrived in Belgrade, the most sought-after person in the city was a woman named Mila Damianova. Dr. Dabić was head over heels in love with her, according to those who knew the couple.

"We used to go to conferences and symposia together," says Tatiana Jovanović from a publication called *Healthy Life*. "Dabić never took his eyes off her. They always sat next to each other, and they spent the breaks hugging and stroking each other's hands."

"I often saw them together, holding hands," says Milica Sener, a neighbor of Dr. Dabić. "A polite lady, though I did sometimes wonder, 'What does a young woman like that see in such an old-timer?' But my husband said that after the war in Serbia there were too few men. Better an old one than none at all."

I too went looking for Mila among the high-rise apartment

blocks in Belgrade's Zemun district. In vain, until Mila turned up of her own accord. She gave an interview to a Serbian tabloid called *Press*. "I disappeared first because I wanted to explain to Mr. Karadžić's family that I was never his lover. Only when I was sure the information had reached Mrs. Karadžić did I agree to do this interview.

"Who was I? A woman fascinated by the man's deep wisdom and spirituality. Dr. Dabić was immensely knowledgeable about mysticism but also about art, philosophy, and history. But the relationship between us was never what I might call intimate."

Now there's a new theory about Mila on the streets of Belgrade: from the very start she was an agent for the special services, whose job it was to expose Karadžić.

The Karadžić pancake

"Ladies and gentlemen, now we're going to the Pinocchio pancake house. He ate there several times a week. Usually something sweet. Now they've created a pancake in his memory: Nutella, walnuts, and cranberries. Look, it's here in writing—see that? 'Radovan Karadžić—150 dinars.' What do I think about it? These days everyone's trying to find a way to earn a living. What's wrong with that? One restaurant set out a chair in the middle of the room with a sign saying 'President Karadžić sat here.' Another introduced some vegetarian dishes under the heading 'Doctor Karadžić recommends.'"

The tour guide also shows us, posted in the window of the Pinocchio pancake house, a newspaper article about the fact that Karadžić used to eat there. Next to it, a famous Serbian tennis player praises the chicken pancakes. The staff say the Karadžić pancake goes over very well. For the tour guide, it's yet more proof that this is a real gold mine.

"Ladies and gentlemen, we also tried to persuade the people at his apartment block to have one of them dress up as Dr. Dabić for our tour. He'd put on a false beard and a black sweater. He could have charged one euro for a photo. But they don't want to do it. They haven't got that sort of business mind-set yet. Communism is still uppermost in their minds."

A package deal works out cheaper

"I hope you've enjoyed our tour. Unfortunately, it isn't available to individual clients. We only include it as part of our Belgrade sightseeing program. Each group can choose from Tito's, Tesla's (Tesla was our great inventor), or Karadžić's Belgrade. You can also get a package deal, Tesla and Karadžić for example. A package deal works out cheaper.

"At the end of our tour, we have a surprise for you. We're driving past the state prosecution building where Mr. Karadžić ended up immediately after his arrest. You'll be able to take a picture. Of course I'll take one of me and you! You people from Japan are always so nice.

"Here's the prosecution building. This is where Mr. Dabić was given a haircut and became Mr. Karadžić again. From here he was taken to the airport, and then on to the Hague.

"Where should I stand? Here? Great! All together now: 'Serbia!' Snap! Done.

"The tour? Most people respond well to it. They want to see the places associated with Mr. Karadžić. We answer to that demand.

"Just one lady wrote to say she didn't like the name Pop Art

Radovan. She said that people will start to perceive Mr. Karadžić as a sympathetic figure—as a nice old-timer with a long beard, in slightly oversized glasses. She wanted us to call the tour War Criminal Karadžić. Well, tell me honestly—would you have gone on a tour called that?

"But that lady probably doesn't know how to run a tourist agency. Besides, apparently she lost a loved one in the war. That sort of experience changes people a lot.

"But there you go getting me off the point again. We just want to promote Serbia, its culture and hospitality. There's a demand for this sort of tour, so we organize them."

Serbia: Chickens for the Serbs

We're racing toward Priština in a Honda four-by-four. The driver is Florent, an Albanian. Beside him sits Dušan, a Serb. Both are from Mitrovica, where the Serb-Albanian conflict is at its most heated. I'm nervously waiting to see what will happen along the way. Will they quarrel? Fight? Shoot? Nothing of the kind.

"How is it possible for you two guys to be sitting next to each other in the same car?" I finally ask.

"We hate each other. But the price of gas is really high," says Florent, and both he and Dušan burst out laughing. "Get lost or I'll slug you . . . ," splutters Dušan.

"We've known each other since we were kids," he finally explains. "We used to play soccer together before there was any sign that Yugoslavia would disintegrate. My parents lived in the Albanian part of the city. I've still got lots of friends there now."

"Serbs have Albanian friends?" I ask to be sure. They say yes. Could I have met a more curious double act in the entire country?

Watch out for Mercedes cars

Everyone advised me against hitchhiking in Kosovo. "The Kosovars drive like maniacs. They're tearaways, and they always try to milk tourists down to their last euro," claimed the foreigners with whom I had a cup of coffee just after flying into Priština.

"The UN has spoiled them terribly," said the first. "They're giving them heaps of money for everything. I don't believe anyone'll drive you half a mile for free."

"In the best case, you come upon a cheat. In the worst, they put you out in your socks in the middle of a minefield," sniggered another.

"Watch out for Mercedes cars with tinted windows," added the third. "Mafia. They might sell you for your organs."

I didn't believe a word of it. It was February 2008; just a few days earlier Kosovo had declared independence, and I wanted to see the Kosovars at this important moment in their history. I wanted to take a close look at them only days after their country became the youngest in Europe—drink their coffee, eat their bread, laugh at their jokes, and ride in their cars. And so it was that one February morning I came to be standing on the hard shoulder of the highway from Priština to Peja.

I was probably the first hitchhiker in independent Kosovo.

Trash, scrap metal, and good advice

Kosovo is a very strange place. Take the cell phones. In half an hour I'm welcomed by networks from three different countries. First of all Monaco, because that particular country once won a tender here. And as Kosovo has no area code of its own, here they use the principality's number.

Two hours later, as I come close to the border with Macedonia, I'm greeted by the network from over there. On the way I pass a Serbian enclave and am welcomed by a Serbian network.

The whole country is covered in trash. The locals are in the habit of tossing it straight into the river. Apparently, there used to be a river flowing through Priština, but it became so polluted that the authorities had it cemented over and built a housing development on top of it.

This does have its good sides. Throughout my time in Kosovo, my hay fever disappeared. There aren't many trees, and the grass is rather sparse too. The typical landscape is a big pile of trash, a mile or so of scrap heaps, and another pile of trash.

In just this sort of place—between a car wash, a scrap heap, and a gas station—I try to hitch a ride. I start waving a hand rather timidly. The string of speeding cars doesn't even slow down. I wave more boldly. Still nothing. Some of the drivers speed up at the sight of me. Apparently, that's a habit left over from the war: something weird—run for it!

Others stare at me as if I were a strange species of animal. Old geezers in Albanian hats shaped like half an egg smile in a friendly way. Someone takes a picture with his cell phone. But nobody stops.

Oh well, so hitchhiking isn't popular around here. Every man's ambition is to have his own car. "I might not have the money for food, but I'll always find it for gas," one of the drivers tells me a few days later.

A column of army trucks and two amphibious vehicles go past me. A boy comes up from the gas station and explains in broken German—I think everyone in Kosovo knows that language—that the bus station is less than five hundred yards from here. "Why don't you hire a car?" he asks. "Because I want to meet people," I reply. "What for?" he says, shaking his head in disbelief, and goes back to work.

A little later a black Mercedes with tinted windows stops. Just like the ones I'm told the Mafia ride around in. My heart leaps to my throat.

Executions

"Europe and rest of the world know nothing about Kosovo," a Kosovar I'd befriended told me. "All you people know is where it is, and in which year the war happened. Apart from that, you can be persuaded of anything. You think bombs explode here every day of the week, and the women go around dressed like in Afghanistan. Meanwhile it's a normal country, like in Europe, just a bit poorer."

Then we talked for a while about Kosovar drivers. Despite the stories, they drive fairly calmly and safely.

"The police punished the road hogs with a public flogging. Several of the most dangerous were shot," he said with a stony face. I was horrified. We sat for a while in silence, until my friend couldn't keep it up and snorted with laughter.

"You see, didn't I say you people will believe anything?"

Priština to Peja: there's no inspection, but there is business

The driver of the black Mercedes is called Mërgim. Mafia? He smiles broadly and points a finger at the car wash. "That's the real mafia."

I don't understand. By now I know the first driver isn't going to sell my kidneys on the black market. I'm already sprawling comfortably on the leather upholstery. But I still don't know what the guys clutching a bit of rubber hose have in common with the Mafia, which earns a fortune from smuggling.

Mërgim, a young businessman in a gray track suit, laughs at me. "You see the car wash on the right? I know the owner. He drives a Maybach. I have a furniture factory. I employ two hundred people. He has a car wash. He only employs his brother-in-law."

"I don't get it . . ."

"It's a money-laundering outfit! The guy does some business on the black market and pays the money into a bank. The inspector comes along and asks, 'Where did you get a million dollars from?' And he says, 'I've got a car wash. I work hard. I've washed half a million cars.' Everyone knows it's a scam. But in Kosovo the inspection services are flagging. No one'll do a thing to him."

"What about your factory? Where did you get the idea?"

"I never expected to have a factory. I didn't know I'd ever see Kosovo again. In 1999, when I left with my parents for Germany, it was a complete pit. My father worked in Priština, as a translator for one of the foreign newspapers. He got us the right to stay in Bonn. I finished school there and started working for a German. He was an extremely rich and resourceful guy. We became friends. One day I was going to visit my family. He asked me, 'Mërgim, perhaps you'd look around for some business? Maybe there's money to be earned there?'

"So I went, and started asking around. I thought we'd open a store or a bar. I found out that a large furniture factory in Peja was standing empty. It was for sale at half price, providing that you employed people. I asked the German, 'Should we take it?' To which he said, 'I've never made furniture!' So I said, 'Neither have I. But these people have.' These days we're selling our products to Greece, Macedonia, and Serbia. And to Germany, of course."

"Is it profitable?"

"And how! Kosovars will work for two hundred euros a month.* These days this is a country of incredible opportunities. Do you know how much cash has been pumped into this place over the past nine years? The UN alone has contributed almost thirty billion euros. On top of that there's the EU and the charities. I once counted it up. For every square mile they've put in five billion euros. But even so the investors were afraid to come in here. Now that's coming to an end. Since independence was declared, a huge number of people have been calling me. They want to invest. They can see there's a market here. Outside Gjakova there are about a dozen factories. They're still empty, but I know half of them have already been bought by Turks."

We stop in the center of Peja. There's a building that looks like a UFO. In the downtown area, situated on a small river, there's nothing but youth. Not surprising—well over half the Kosovars are under thirty.

Hotel Begolli: there's no apartheid, but there is a Jacuzzi

The Kosovars from across the border who have prospered are now doing their best to invest as much as possible in the country. One example is the Begolli family hotel, where I stayed in Priština. Practicality imported from Germany combines here with an Albanian fondness for extravagance. An Albanian house must have as many floors as possible. An Albanian hotel has a Jacuzzi in

---

* At the time (February 2008), one euro was worth US$0.67, so two hundred euros was about US$134. Thirty billion euros was about US$20 billion, and five billion euros about US$3.4 billion

every room and tacky, Louis XVI–style furniture. The fact that the Jacuzzi doesn't work and the legs are falling off the chairs is neither here nor there.

A legendary place in Priština is the centrally located Grand Hotel, known as the worst five-star hotel in the world. There are fifteen waiters on duty in the empty restaurant. But if a guest appears, none of them will deign to go up to him.

"Well, it's still a state hotel," sighs Ardita, whom I'm arranging to meet there. "Even so, it's better than it was. There used to be real apartheid here—they only employed Serbs."

"Whereas nowadays there are no Serbs here at all," I add. Ardita simply shrugs.

Prizren to Štrpce: there's no electricity, but there is snow

"I am a Serb. But I have bigger problems on my mind than independence for Kosovo. Such as my roof is leaking. I've no money to repair it. And then there's the electricity . . ."

"The electricity?"

Tatiana is the owner of a shoe store in the Serbian enclave of Štrpce. She picked me up on the road to Prizren. She tells me proudly that no Albanian woman would dare talk to a strange man. That's probably a bit of an exaggeration.

We're riding in her Opel across the Šar Mountains. We pass a KFOR post—KFOR is the NATO-led peacekeeping force. The security of the Serbs is being jointly protected by Ukrainians and Poles. A small Orthodox church on the right-hand side of the road is a sign that we've now entered the enclave.

"The electricity?" Tatiana takes a deep breath. "Look, the people here are sitting around candles. Do you think they're just being romantic? Sometimes there's no electricity for three hours on end, sometimes for five, sometimes all day long. You never know when it's going to be on. I can't do the laundry or take a bath or wash up. And it's really boring too. In winter it gets dark earlier. The electricity goes off, and you sit there in the dark like a complete dope. You don't feel like going to bed. And there's nothing to do either."

"So what do you do?"

"I chat with my husband. Sometimes someone comes by. But mainly it's a sort of lethargy, torpor. Though some people say the reason why there are so many kids in Kosovo is directly related to the lack of electricity. But then, when they suddenly switch it on, you jump to your feet. No matter what time it is. I always wake up when they switch on the supply at night. Some instinct wakes me up. I take a shower, put on the laundry, watch TV. The people in my town are convinced the Albanians only switch off the Serbs' electricity. I tell them, 'I've been to Prizren. There's no electricity there either,' but they never go anywhere. They just sit in Štrpce talking crap."

"Why don't they go anywhere?"

"They're afraid. Twice a week KFOR provides an escort for buses to the border with Serbia and to Gračanica, where there's an Orthodox church and some wholesalers. The Albanians throw stones at the buses, sometimes firecrackers too. I have a car with Kosovar registration plates, so I'm not afraid. They cost me fifteen hundred euros. But if I had an accident, I don't know what would happen. I don't know a word of Albanian."

"Are you afraid of the Albanians?"

"Are you crazy? I'm only afraid of extremists. My grandpa's best friend is Albanian. They worked together in the mountains. One fine day they slashed their palms with a knife, pressed them together, and became blood brothers. I don't know how they came up with that idea, because there's no such tradition among us. They probably saw it in a western. But from then on we've been like a family. Memed, my grandpa's friend, was the master of ceremonies at my wedding. When the Serbian army was on the rampage in Kosovo, we hid two of his sons. Later on, when the Albanian resistance took revenge, we lived at Memed's. Grandpa is no longer alive, but Memed is doing fine. He has a store in a town a few miles away from here. I always stop by to see him when I go there for shoes. I love him like one of the family. Though I do have one small problem with him."

"What's that?"

"He spoils my kids like mad. A day at Memed's and I can't get them to behave."

"What does Memed think about the Serbs in Kosovo?"

"He can tell the difference between criminals and regular people. Wars are not fought between races. They're fought between criminals from one side and the other. He understands that. After the declaration of independence, he could see that I was out of sorts. 'Tatiana,' he said, 'we're just pawns on the chessboard. The Americans are playing against the Russkies. It's sheer chance that you're a black pawn and I'm a white one.'"

"What about your Serbian neighbors? How do they regard your friendship?"

"They say, 'You're possessed by the devil.' Every day at 12:44 they protest against Kosovar independence. That's in memory of a UN resolution, number 1244, which ruled out independence. And then, as they walk through the city, they scowl at me, because I buy shoes from the Albanians, when I should be boycotting their goods. But as soon as those old crones' Serbian shoes fall apart, they find their way to me. They're gradually getting used to it. Right near here is Brezovica, Kosovo's one and only ski resort.

There's no one but Serbs living there too. After the declaration of independence, they shouted in the streets and burned flags. The Albanians took fright and stopped going there. The skiing conditions are excellent, but the slopes are completely empty.

"These days Brezovica is a quiet place, hopefully waiting for the Albanians to get over it. And I'm hoping the Albanian government will carry out its promises and we'll finally have some electricity. As long as we do, it's all the same to me if the prime minister is a Serb, an Albanian, or a Papuan."

Peja to Gjakova: there are no payments, but there are generators

Kosovo only has one power station. It's located just beyond Priština, and it breaks all possible environmental standards. Apparently, 500 million euros has already been invested in its modernization. Without effect.

Stefan, who works for one of the nongovernmental organizations, gives me a ride toward Gjakova. "The power station has no chance, because nobody's in the habit of paying for electricity here. In the days of Yugoslavia they didn't have to pay, and now it's very hard to teach them to do it. The owner of the apartment I rent is a lawyer. When I show him the electricity bills, he just laughs and says: '*Mir, mir*—all right, all right.'

"At the same time, everyone buys a small generator. Every little store, every barbershop or café, has one. When they switch off the electricity, all over town you can hear a constant *trrrr*. It costs far more than the electricity bills. But you can't persuade anyone otherwise.

"The power station can't cut off the people who don't pay—it would have to cut off the entire block. When there turned out to be entire blocks where no one pays, the power station employees came by. They took a real beating.

"The power station only survives by selling electricity to Macedonia. For several hours the supply to the whole of Kosovo is switched off, and they send it all across the border."

Prizren to Dragaš: there's no parsley

The Kosovars rather disparagingly refer to their Albanian brothers as "the elite in shoes full of holes."

The Albanians refer to the Kosovars as grasping swindlers.

The Kosovars regard themselves as richer. The Albanians regard themselves as wiser.

Asked whether Kosovo will unite with Albania, both the former and the latter will sidestep an unambiguous answer.

"We've lived apart for too long. We're too different to unite," says a minibus driver outside Prizren.

But there's a small flag with a black Albanian eagle hanging in his car. He doesn't regard the flag of Kosovo, blue with six little stars, as his own.

Lars, a Dane with whom I'm traveling about the Gora region, has his own theory on the subject. "It'd be hard for them to unite. They're extremely different. I was in Albania recently. As soon as they have a bit of lake, a hundred people immediately start dealing in fish. If there's a stream flowing down from the mountains, a hundred boys will be standing by the road to wash your car. But in Kosovo they just sit on their butts, waiting for help to come to them of its own accord. And it does. These people don't have to do anything for themselves—they live on aid from humanitarian organizations and from their cousins in Germany. The Serbs here are maintained by the government in Belgrade. It gives them money as long as they don't leave the place. Have you been to Štrpce? Several thousand Serbs live there. The hospital in a town like that should employ at most thirty people. It employs over three hundred. Half of them don't even go to work, and their salaries are three times higher than for the hospital workers in Belgrade. But even so, the UN is the worst of all."

"Why?"

"They overpay for everything. A relative employed at the UN can calmly support a family of ten. If they can do that, why bother to farm the land? Take a look, it's all lying fallow. Nobody feels like doing it."

"You're exaggerating. They have 70 percent unemployment here. Most people live on one euro a day."

"Those are statistics. But they don't even bother to grow parsley for themselves."

Gjakova to Baljak: there's peace; there will be chickens

The Honda four-by-four picks me up outside Gjakova. This is where I meet Florent and Dušan, the two old friends from Mitrovica.

"So what's Serbian-Albanian friendship like?" I ask, because I find it hard to believe them. "I thought you guys were only capable of beating each other up."

"Not true. As kids we had fights between neighboring yards, but not Albanians against Serbs. Whenever my parents went away somewhere, I stayed the night at a Serbian pal's house. I know both languages extremely well," says Florent.

"But you speak Albanian with a hick accent," says Dušan, and both jokers burst out laughing again.

"It was only in the 1980s, when Milošević took autonomy away from Kosovo, that things started to heat up. After that, they just got hotter. Dušan's parents swapped houses with some Albanians living on the Serbian side. Everyone went to ground in their own ghettoes."

"We didn't see each other from 1996 to 2000. We were both working for NGOs, when one day we were both at the same meeting in Belgrade. Florent asked if I wanted to come work with him. So we've been working together for an organization called Partners Kosova. I'm the only Serb here."

"We're driving to work together. There's no other way to do it, because Dušan's car has Serbian plates."

"Meaning?"

"His registration number has the initials KM. That stands for Kosovska Mitrovica, and those plates are issued by Belgrade."

"Where I live, everyone has those plates."

"But in Priština they might smash your windows or beat you up if you have number plates like those. My plates have KS, meaning Kosovo. We drive to work with them. But if I go to visit with Dušan, I leave my KS car by the New Bridge in Mitrovica and switch into Dušan's car." The New Bridge separates the Serbian and Albanian districts.

"In the Serbian part of town you can get a punch on the nose for KS plates."

The Honda with KS plates turns off the highway and stops in the village of Baljak. There are a dozen half-built houses made of red brick. On the edge of the village there's a small mosque and an even smaller Orthodox church. The local community leader has requested chickens for the Serbs. Why? He can tell us himself. We pick up the community leader from his house and drive to the administration office, which the UN has built for the village.

"As community leader I'm very pleased we've won our independence. The authorities in our village are doing everything they can for coexistence to . . . ," the community leader starts to say.

"Osman, we don't have the time. Cut the oration," says Florent, laughing.

"You're right. I'm prattling like a politician." The community leader laughs too.

"So why is it that the Serbs need chickens?" I ask.

"Until 2004 there wasn't a single Serb left in our village. They'd all run off with the army. They were afraid we'd take revenge on them. But now time has passed and not all of them have made a life for themselves in Serbia. Now Belgrade is protesting against our independence, but they don't treat the Serbs from Kosovo well there. So they're starting to come back. In the past four years twelve families have returned—almost fifty people. The UN gives us money. We're building houses for them. We're helping them to get set up. But it's not enough, because they don't have jobs. So we had the idea of giving them chickens. They'll be starting up miniature farms, selling eggs and meat. They'll have something to eat. We've bought a small hut for one of them, and he'll have a greengrocer's store there. Tomorrow we're going to fetch the first hundred chickens. Maybe this will allow us to attract a few more Serbs."

"Why would you want to do that?"

"So the government in Belgrade won't go saying they're badly treated here. Besides, there's money provided for it. Why not take advantage of that?"

"Aren't the Albanians protesting?"

"I have a neighbor. A great Albanian patriot. Ask him about the Serbs, he'd say he'd shoot the lot. But when they started to come back, it reminded him that he used to have a good friend called Goran, who was a Serb. And now he runs after me to ask if I can get his pal Goran to come back. Because he'd like to see him again before he dies."

VIII. Castration

But any bear that's been a captive for most of its life has no chance of coping with freedom. . . . That's why we decided that we have to sterilize all our bears.

Georgia: Stalin's Vestal Virgins

He comes to me at night. He gazes at me, puffs on his pipe, and twirls his mustache. He smiles, and then heads for the door. Then I weep and cry for him to stay. But what guy would be bothered by a woman crying? Georgian men are like that: they have a drink, enter you, come quickly, and fall asleep. I hate men who drink. But here in Gori there's no other kind. The other kind only exists in American movies.

"Stalin was a different matter. Highly civilized. He knew how to take care of a woman, how to pay her a compliment, how to smell nice. He lived modestly, but he wore smart clothes. And he didn't drink too much. And if he did, it was only good, foreign alcohol. I hardly need mention the fact that he conquered fascism and Hitler. So I said to myself many years ago, 'Tanya, why the hell should you have to squabble with drunks? Why the hell, when you can live with Stalin?'"

Anna Sreseli: he's like family

"We're standing outside the house where Joseph Vissario-novich Stalin was born. His parents lived in poverty. His mother did laundry for the local priests. His father was a cobbler. As you can see, his house has had a structure in the classical style built around it, and the neighboring ones have been demolished. Yes, the entire district. No, I don't think there's anything odd about that. Would you be happier if there were hens crapping here, and children playing ball?

"My grandmother lived in one of the houses that was de-molished. She was given an apartment in a block. To the end of her life she kept saying, 'How happy I am to have been born next to Stalin's house. And that I can still see it from my windows.'

"Grandmother could remember Stalin's mother. He lived here for more than a decade. She lived here almost to the end of her life. For us, it was a big source of pride. The biggest. Because in our town there's nothing else going on. If it weren't for the museum, the town would have ceased to exist long ago.

"A few years ago we had a war. The Ossetia border isn't far away. A hundred Russian tanks drove into Gori. We fled to Tbilisi. I wasn't afraid they'd blow up my housing block and my apart-ment, only that they'd blow up the museum. But they didn't dam-age anything. They're still afraid of Stalin. They didn't touch the smallest patch of grass. They just took photos of each other by his statue. And that's how Stalin saved us from beyond the grave.

"When I was at school, some of the girls dreamed of work-ing in a store, others longed to fly into outer space, but I wanted to tell people about our great compatriot. I steered my entire life toward making it come true. I chose to study history. And after college I ran straight to the museum to ask for a job.

"But by then the Soviet Union had collapsed. The museum

was closed and had barely survived. They had only recently be-gun to employ people again. I was the first person to be accepted in the new intake. Meanwhile I'd started to teach history at the high school—so I work part time at the museum.

"When I was at college, we were still taught that Stalin was an outstanding statesman. But the system changed, the curriculum changed, and now I have to teach that he was a tyrant and a crimi-nal. I don't think that's true. The resettlements? They were neces-sary for people to live in peace. The killings? He wasn't responsible for them—it was Beria. The famine in Ukraine? That was a natural disaster. The Katyn massacre? I knew you'd ask. All the Poles ask about it. But there was a war on—in wartime that sort of action is a normal thing. And before you start ranting, please let me finish. Are you feeling calmer now? All right, I'll tell you my personal opinion.

"I regard Stalin as a great man, but I can't say that, either to my students or to the tourists, so I say, 'Some regard him as a dictator, others as a tyrant, and others see him as a genius. What he really was, you can decide for yourselves.'"

Tatiana Mardzhanishvili: O Christ, take me to dear Stalin

"When I see what they've done to our beloved Stalin, my heart bleeds! How could they? How could they make such a good man into a monster, a cannibal, an ogre?

"Once upon a time, bus after bus came to our museum. Peo-ple stood in lines several hundred yards long. I used to look at those people's faces, and I could see the goodness emanating from them. But nowadays? One would bite the other. That's capitalism for you.

"Now I don't go there anymore. First, because of regret—for

my youth, my job, and my friends. And second, because my legs are weak. I can't even get down the stairs on my own. In March I'll be eighty-two, and you can't expect a person to be healthy all their life. In the morning I get up, cut a slice of bread, make the tea, sit down, and say to myself, 'O Christ, why did you let me live to see times like these? Why do they badmouth our darling Stalin?'

"But later I think, 'Just remember, Tanya, how much Stalin suffered for the people. It was for you too that he went without enough food and sleep. He fought against fascism so you could finish your education.' And then I fetch the medal with Stalin's face on it, which I was given when I retired. I stroke the darling man's mustache, and somehow I feel better.

"I worked at the museum from 1975. As a *nabliudatel*, a person responsible for the order and safety of the exhibits. If anyone tried to touch them, we had to go and shout at them.

"It wasn't easy. Old women used to come from the villages and throw themselves at our Stalin. They had to kiss each picture in the display, like icons in a church. And there are over a thousand of those pictures! If a whole busload of those old crones drove in, and they all wanted to kiss them, what was I to do? If the director was looking, I'd go up and shout. But if he wasn't, I'd say, 'Kiss away, ladies. May God grant you good health! But don't touch the mask! Under no circumstances.' The mask is the most sacred object in the entire museum, because it's his death mask.

"Before, I worked at the National Museum in Tbilisi, but my second husband was from Gori, and I managed to arrange a transfer. It wasn't easy. The Stalin museum wasn't a place you could just walk into off the street and ask, 'You don't have a job opening, do you?' Public opinion counted. I was a divorcée. My first husband drank and beat me—the less said about him the better. At the time, I was afraid the divorce would be a problem. Luckily, I had a very good reference from the museum in Tbilisi.

"The smartest people from all over the world used to come and admire Stalin's house. From all over Russia, Asia, and America. Journalists, ambassadors, and artists. And I stood among the exhibits with a small card showing my name, as proud as could be. That job meant everything to me. The museum was like a home to me.

"My husband didn't understand. I had nothing to talk to him about. Although I only guarded the exhibits, I used to read books and got to know new people. But he drank too. He tried to beat me, but this time I wasn't having it. Later on, he fell sick and went on welfare. He'd spend all day long sitting in the apartment, or at his mother's. He used to say nasty things about Stalin, just to spite me.

"When the USSR collapsed, he stuck out his tongue at me. It gave him great satisfaction. And then he died.

"It's a shame he didn't live to the present times. Now I'd be sticking out my tongue at him. What do we need all this capitalism for, all these American cheeses, juices, and chocolate? You can't even buy normal milk anymore—it has to be in a carton, because that's how it is in America. I think, 'O Christ, take me off to my dear Stalin. Take me away from this world, because I can't bear it here any longer.'"

Nana Magavariani: whenever I see him, a shiver goes down my spine

"My job title used to be 'head of personnel.' Nowadays it's 'manager.'

"The museum has a total of sixty-three employees. I am responsible for their recruitment and employment. There are ten tour guides, eleven custodians, and two cashiers. Since last year, we also have a pioneer—a girl in a uniform and a red scarf who sells postcards and poses for pictures. That was my idea, for which I received a personal commendation from the director. 'A tourist has to have something to be photographed with, sir. Otherwise he won't praise our museum, and as a result we'll have bad PR.' I know, because we've had special training on tourist activity within capitalism.

"In the past, people used to come mainly from the Soviet Union. Russian was enough for us, but we also had two ladies who knew English and French. Nowadays a Russian tourist is a rare occasion for celebration. If one turns up, half the personnel comes to look at him. And we give him the best possible tour. Let them see that politics is politics, but the Georgians are their friends.

"These days most of the tourists are from America and Poland. And that's a problem, because not all the ladies know English well enough to provide for that sort of tourist—here each tourist has a personal guide. What can we do? It's not as if I'm going to fire the ladies before their retirement, or teach them English. They can see that in the new times they're not needed, and that they're a sort of burden for the museum. But we never talk to one another about it. I know what it means to lose your job in your prime.

"I used to work at a clothing factory. In the personnel department too. When the Soviet Union collapsed, the factory collapsed with it. And everything was looted—even the glass was stolen out of the window frames. In Stalin's day something like that wouldn't have been possible. The culprits would have been punished. So these days when I hear the stories they tell about him, I say,

'People, you've lost your minds. Remember the Soviet Union. Everyone had work. The children had a free education. From Tbilisi to Vladivostok.' If it weren't for Communism, I, for example, would still be living in the countryside. I would never have thought of occupying a managerial position, because only men had those jobs before then. No system has ever given women as much.

"Since its collapse, everything is worse. In the past, the doctors couldn't refuse to help a poor person. Now the health service is private, and even if you break a leg you have to pay. It's the same with education. A retired person used to have the phone for free, and paid less for electricity. But now? You get a pension of twenty dollars, and the prices are like in the West.

"And life gets worse and worse for women. In the USSR men had a good life. There were no wars. And if a man hit you, you could go and complain to the party committee. The committee informed the party cell at the factory, and the abuser could get into big trouble.

"These days the men have no work and they're frustrated. And when one of them hits you, you've no one to defend you.

"But at our museum most of the staff are women. Even in the support services, which I haven't encountered at any other workplace of this kind. Most of the space here is dedicated to Stalin as a son, a husband, and a father. Less to him as a soldier or as a strategist. Women are much better suited to this.

"I also think Stalin's magic is at work here. Women were always mad about him. The wives of diplomats wrote in their diaries that he was very attractive.

"Something of his charm remains to this day. Sometimes when I stop at his death mask, I only have to glance at it, and it sends such a shiver down my spine that I have to go outside into the fresh air for a while."

Larisa Gazashvili: I love his poetry

"My parents were the Romeo and Juliet of the Stalin era.

"My paternal grandfather was a Georgian prince. He rode a white horse, he had a large estate, and in his house he kept a padlocked chest of gold. When Communism came along, they called him a kulak,* they took away his land and his gold, and left him with nothing but the chest. I still have it to this day.

"My maternal grandfather was from a peasant family. Thanks to Stalin, he went to school. Thanks to Stalin, he worked on a collective farm, and later on—also thanks to Stalin—he became its manager.

"The worse life became for my paternal grandfather, the better it was for my maternal one. When my parents fell in love, neither of their fathers would hear of them getting married.

"My grandfather, the manager, shut my mother in the house under lock and key. Later on he sent her to college in Moscow. He sought out suitors for her among the sons of his friends.

"My other grandfather, the prince, sought a wife for my father from the former aristocracy. Later on he shouted at him. And even later he cursed him.

"But as we all know, when young people dig in their heels there's no one more determined. My parents got married, with neither set of parents present at the wedding. They never went to visit each other, and pretended not to know each other. So it was to the end of their lives.

"So when I got a job at the Stalin museum, my grandfather

---

* A farmer characterized by the Communists as having excessive wealth and as a result denounced as an oppressor of less fortunate farmers and subjected to severe penalties.

the manager kissed me heartily. And my grandfather the prince was mortally offended.

"At the museum I was responsible for propaganda. It was a very serious role. We used to publish a newspaper, Stalin's poetry, and other literature. He wrote beautiful poems. Romantic, tugging at the heartstrings. If he hadn't become a politician, who knows, maybe he'd have won the Nobel Prize?

"The newspaper was called *Bulletin*. Or rather at one time it was called *Bulletin of the Joseph Vissarionovich Stalin Museum*. But when the Soviet Union collapsed, it was reduced to *Bulletin*. To avoid hurting anyone's feelings.

"When the USSR collapsed, we had awful confusion. First they closed our museum; then they opened it again. They changed the exhibition, then went back to the old one. Nobody had the money to replace the entire display. Nor did anyone have the courage to close the museum down entirely. Too many Georgians still love Stalin.

"Now, unfortunately, there's no money to publish the *Bulletin*. And I'm a tour guide.

"I went to college in Kaliningrad. I had a good life there. I worked at a school, but when Mommy fell seriously ill I had to come back to Gori.

"Some people we knew said a woman at the Stalin museum had gone on maternity leave. So I went to the party committee to ask about the job. They said first I had to pass an exam.

"The exam was hard. I had to quote by heart from the history of the Communist Party, Stalin's biography, and the history of the USSR. But I had studied history. I knew it all by heart. So I passed with flying colors.

"So many bad things are said about Communism, but in the past the director understood that on Sundays I had to have the day off because I'm a churchgoer. Yet now they've put me down for Sundays. Out of malice, I'm sure."

Tatiana Gurgenidze: I'd have been good to him

"I was born in a bad system. Because I have the mentality of a socialist hero of labor. When something needs to be done for society, I go and do it. I've produced a wall newspaper for the employees and classes for single mothers bringing up children on their own.

"In the Communist era, everyone would have respected me. But now that we have capitalism, they look at me as if I'm an idiot.

"So when I really can't manage anymore, I come to the museum to calm down. And I say, 'Mr. Stalin, I know you'd appreciate it.' And it helps. And when I dream about Stalin—as I told you, he looks at me, twirls his moustache, and leaves—it's usually a few days after one of those relaxing museum visits.

"I'm not really in the right era when it comes to my attitude to men either. You see, there wasn't any sex in the Soviet Union, at least not obviously. There was 'intercourse between the genders.' There wasn't any of what the young people watch on television these days. All those music videos and naked butts, if you'll pardon the expression. Instead of a kiss, someone just lightly stroked someone else's arm, and that was enough. A woman had to be a good worker, dress and behave modestly. So whenever I'm shocked by the sight of today's young girls, I go to the museum too. And I say, 'Mr. Stalin, you wouldn't like it either.' And once again it helps.

"I don't like drunks. Or drug addicts. Our president upsets me, because why does he have to antagonize Russia? It's a known fact that you can even come to terms with a bear if you want to. But

Saakashvili* is insistent—with Russia just across the border—on making a second America here. We've had a war because of him, and we're sure to have another one too. When the war was on, they closed the museum, so I came to the park, to the statue, and I said, 'Mr. Stalin, you'd have got a firm grip on it all, and there'd be peace.'

"And sometimes I go and say to him, 'If you were alive, maybe we'd be together. You'd have a good time with me. I know how to cook, I'm a cheerful person, and I can sing well too.' And I fantasize about how nice it would be to be Stalin's wife. But later on I reject those thoughts, because I'm behaving like an idiot. Stalin is dead. Communism has collapsed. It's over. It's finished. Been and gone.

"If I dream about him when I'm feeling like that, I'm very cold and official toward him in my dream."

Natia Joldbori: son, be like Stalin

"My momma told me, 'Darling, don't go for that job. Of course Stalin was a great man. But something like that looks bad on your résumé these days. One day you'll want a different job, and they won't give it to you. Besides, it's embarrassing to work there.'

"But I have a small son, and I needed the money. In Gori, if you have any ambitions, there's no choice. You can teach at a school or work in the local administration. Or at Stalinland—that's what some people call our museum. Young people especially like to make fun of it. They call the women who work here the Stalinettes or the vestal virgins—because it's as if they're doing their best not to let the flame of Communism go out. I keep all that at arm's length, though I can see that for most people in Gori the world ended when the

---

* Mikheil Saakashvili was president of Georgia from 2004 to 2013.

USSR collapsed. I have one elderly colleague whose grandfathers were both killed in the Stalin era, but even so she'll never stop defending him and loving him.

"I can hardly remember Communism. I was born when it was in its decline. I remember seeing the tanks in Vilnius on TV. When we regained independence, my dad and I went to the main town square with a Georgian flag. Those are fine memories.

"Dad soon understood the new times. He sent me to learn English when I was just seven years old. Thanks to my English, I got my job at the museum. There are only two of us here who can speak it. As a result, we have the most tour groups, while the ladies who are deeply in love with Stalin sit and make themselves cup after cup of coffee. Afterward, we get the same salary as them. But I'm not complaining. The main thing is that I have a job.

"My son doesn't know a single word of Russian. He's had English since preschool. It'll be a totally different generation. Stalin? A completely abstract concept.

"What do I think about Stalin? Here, in Gori, it's customary for parents or grandparents to take their kids to the museum and tell them about him. I brought my toddler here too. And I told him, just like it says in those American guides to success, 'He was much worse off than you are. His father drank, his cottage was falling down, and the other kids were good-for-nothings. But he was hardworking, thanks to which years later he ruled the entire country. If you study, you can achieve a lot too.'"

Anna Tkabladze: we boycott the carve-up of Poland

"Here we have his favorite cigarettes. Here's the watch he was given by his mother. He was a good son. An affectionate husband. A loving father. He cared for his staff as if they were his own children.

"Nowadays they say he was a bad man. But in the archive we have pictures of him planting apple trees in the summer. I think a bad man would have been beating someone up or killing them, not planting trees. You have your views. That he murdered millions. But there's no proof of that. All the documents were faked by Beria. Stalin only made one mistake—he was too good. He put too much trust in others.

"I can't say all that to the tourists. The management writes scripts for the guided tours. What's in them? Just like I said: he was a good son and an affectionate husband. We can also mention that he defeated fascism. But not much more. Murders? I've just about had enough of you. Here we have a sort of unwritten agreement that if a tourist really gets under our skin, we can go outside the museum to argue with him. But right now we are inside the museum, and I have to stick to the script.

"They've even posted a sign about the Ribbentrop-Molotov Pact. Of course, it was wrong from the start. Because for Poland it certainly wasn't a good pact at all. But it gave the USSR a few years to arm itself, thanks to which fascism was defeated. But we're supposed to give the impression that the carve-up of Poland was a myth. So we leave that sign out of our tours. It's our silent boycott.

"I'll tell you frankly, I don't know what to think about the Poles. On the one hand, when we had the war with Russia here, you people helped us a lot. Trucks full of clothes and food kept arriving every day.

"But nobody harps on us as much as you people. Everyone else comes through here and listens with interest, but the Poles shout at me as if I were Stalin himself and had carved up Poland in person. And now they're saying Poland is going to help rebuild the Stalin Museum as the Museum of the Fight against Communism. If that's true, all Gori will come to a standstill. Because we have nothing here except for our Stalin."

IX. Dancing Bears

When they see a human being, they stand up on their hind legs and start rocking from side to side. As if they were begging, as in the past, for bread, candy, a sip of beer, a caress, or to be free of pain. Pain that nobody has been inflicting on them for years.

Greece: We'll Sweep Capitalism Away

Because the government is cutting our salaries but not their own. Because the Germans have made Greece into a farm. They're earning billions here, but they won't stop criticizing us.

Because we didn't invent democracy just to have someone make all the decisions behind our backs.

Because capitalism is crap. We've started a landslide that's going to sweep it away.

It's March 2010, and for a few weeks now the center of Athens has been blockaded nonstop by demonstrators. Teachers, nurses, shipyard workers, engineers, and anarchists. Storekeepers shoulder to shoulder with gas-pump attendants. Pencil pushers side by side with punks. "Instead of tightening their belts, they've all come out onto the streets in jubilant mood," says Jacek, who runs an import-export firm in Greece. "The ship known as Greece is sinking. The government is trying to save it: it has raised VAT and the price of gas, and has cut posts and bonuses in the state sector. But instead of cooperating, the Greeks are holding a general strike. And more millions of euros are going down the drain."

"Why is that?" I ask.

"The southern temperament. In Ireland, people dutifully began to save, and they're getting back on the straight. But the Greeks? They're stubborn. When one of the factories canceled the workers' coffee break, it went bust. That's their character. Anyway, why are you talking to me? Go ask the Greeks. In Athens there's a protest of some kind on every street corner."

Monday, or the hoteliers who bang their heads against the sidewalk

Costas, owner of a small hotel below the Acropolis, hardly sleeps at all these days.

"I've never watched the TV news before. Hell, but it sure sucks you in," he says, stirring sugar into his fourth coffee of the day. "If anyone were to ban me from drinking coffee, I'd go on strike too. But they won't. Going back to the television, the thing that really grabs me is the yellow band at the bottom. 'Rail workers cancel.' 'Inspectors continue.' 'Doctors commence.' 'Sailors suspend.' Cancel and continue what, you say? How do you mean, what? The strike, of course! It's the only thing the guests are asking about. And these days every guest is worth his weight in gold stolen by the Germans."

The Germans have been reproached about the stolen gold by Theodoros Pangalos, Greek deputy prime minister, because they've been criticizing the Greeks for their failure to manage their finances. "Everyone's letting their emotions fly," says Costas, nodding his head with understanding. We're sitting in the summer garden at his small hotel. The apricot trees have just begun to flower. "One lady came here from Germany and said, 'You people have a crisis because you're lazy and deceitful.' I felt like telling her that if they hadn't robbed us during the Second World War, we'd be living like Germans now. But I kept my mouth shut. We can't offend the Germans. Too many of them keep coming here, and nobody knows what's going to happen a month ahead. The customers watch the TV news too. And if there's nothing in it about Greece, then I get twenty phone calls a day and twice as many e-mails inquiring about bookings. But they just have to show some little hoodlums burning tires, and I only get two or three calls and eight e-mails at most. What am I to do? How can I protest? Go outside the hotel and bang my head against the sidewalk? That's all I can think of. We're going to take a real licking over this crisis. One in five Greeks lives off tourists. If they don't come this year, in the fall we'll all be packing our bags to leave."

Tuesday, or bloggers versus drivers

In Syntagma Square some happy, homeless dogs are mooching around the orange trees. In the middle there's an elegant fountain. On the corner there's a McDonald's. On the far side guardsmen with garters and pompoms are guarding the Tomb of the Unknown Soldier. Above it rises the parliament building.

"This is where they rob us," says Maria, a peroxide blonde approaching forty, who works for one of the foreign banks, puffing out her lower lip in disgust. "That's why we're blocking this farce."

During the general strike in early March, more than one hundred thousand people came past here. But the government said it would make deductions from state salaries in response to the strike. Nobody wants to lose their daily rate of pay. So the trade unions decided to organize small protests by sector. "It's better like that," says Maria. "I finish work, take a shower, and arrive here at exactly the moment when there's the biggest tail-back. I work at a private bank, and there's no question of protesting. If my boss saw me at Syntagma Square, I'd be in big trouble. Others are in a similar situation, so we've been making our protest as Greek bloggers."

"What do you do at the bank?"

"I advise clients who have more than a hundred thousand euros."*

"What about you? If you had a hundred thousand euros today, what would you do?"

"I'd get out of Greece. Various weird things are going to happen here. But for now we're banding together on the Internet and urging the government to tax the church and the shipbuilders. Did you know that most of the land in Greece belongs to the church? And that it doesn't pay a single euro for it? It's the same with the shipowners, in other words the richest Greeks."

"And you're protesting against that?"

"Yes. And against rising gasoline prices—from one euro per liter (a quarter of a gallon) it has jumped to one and a half. We're also protesting against the way the government keeps shifting the consequences of its bad political decisions onto the public. My salary won't be reduced. But more expensive gas will affect the price of every last piece of bread and sausage."

The bloggers' protest has only attracted a few dozen people. Nevertheless, Maria is thrilled. "Pretty good for a grassroots initiative."

---

* In March 2010 the euro was worth US$0.74. One hundred thousand euros were worth US$74,000.

Less thrilled are the drivers who are on their way home from work across Syntagma Square. "Walk with us! Gas is too expensive!" shout the protestors, but the only answers they get from behind the steering wheels are insults.

"But Maria, Greece should be tightening its belt!" I try to shout over the car horns.

"Typical propaganda," snaps Maria, puffing out her lower lip again. "Have a talk with Melina. She tightened her belt ten years ago."

Melina is a little over thirty. She teaches biology. Not at one, but at three schools. "I work half time at one high school, a quarter of the time at a second, and an eighth of the time at a third. Why don't I teach anywhere full time? Because although I've been in the profession for ten years, nobody has ever offered me a permanent job!"

"Why not?"

"Getting a permanent job within the Greek state sector is like winning the lottery. You get an annual bonus and they can't fire you. But there are always more job seekers than jobs. So either you have to know someone well or, even better, pay up. As it is, although I've been working in the profession for ten years, I've put almost nothing aside for my retirement. But for the European Union it looks very nice because employment isn't rising."

Not enough nurses

Giorgos, a nurse at a large hospital on the outskirts of Athens, only started putting money aside for his retirement two years ago.

"After twelve years in the job," he stresses. "Because although there's a lack of almost three thousand medical staff in Greece, nobody's bothered about it. And now the government is cutting even more posts and refusing to employ anyone. When our delegation went to see the minister of health, she refused to talk to us—because she was busy receiving a delegation of hospital gardeners."

"But the experts are saying that too many people are employed in your state sector."

"Get your experts to come and see me on night duty. The emergency room is staffed by two doctors and me. And during the night we might have an accident involving two people whose lives need to be saved instantly; a drug addict who's having visions and thinks he's Satan, and whom I have to calm down; a heart-attack victim; and several people with broken bones, whom I dose up with painkillers because I know they're going to have to wait several hours. Meanwhile half the beds in the ward are empty, and we can't make use of all the equipment. Why not? Because of the cuts. Quite often the hospital commissions tests from private hospitals, because then they can be accounted for in a way that looks better in the statistics prepared for the European Union. So what if it costs twice as much? Who's going to worry about that? The Germans are satisfied that we're saving money. And these days that's what matters most."

Wednesday, or shipyard workers versus Germans

"We need to bring the Germans down a peg. That's what we're here for!" says Yannis, who is blocking Omonoia Square.

Omonoia is at the heart of Athens. This is where the main streets and metro lines cross. From here, it's no distance to the Acropolis or to Syntagma Square.

But ever since the district was overrun by illegal immigrants, fewer and fewer indigenous Greeks dare to come here. By day, black men hang around the area, selling fake purses and watches or standing in long lines for soup. By night, prostitutes from Nigeria noisily tout their wares. Here the demonstration by shipyard workers from Piraeus looks a bit like something from another world.

Yannis is fifty-five, and he works at the shipyard as an electrician. Yes, he has heard of Lech Wałęsa—you bet he has. "He's a role model for us, for all Greeks fighting against dictatorship. Except that he fought against a Communist dictatorship, while we're fighting a capitalist one."

I wanted to say that these analogies aren't so obvious at all. But it was hard to interrupt Yannis, who was off on an anti-German diatribe. "They've made Greece into a colony, like in Africa. The whole European Union is a form of colonization. A year ago there was a big scandal, because it turned out Siemens was corrupting Greek officials, and that was how it was winning tenders. The Germans are teaching us how to change our economy, but they're the ones gaining the most from all the loopholes. We bought submarines from them for a vast amount of money."

"And then what?"

"They've broken down! They spin to the left. We call them the 'drunken boats.' The shipyard where I work has been bought by a German too. They were supposed to develop production, so they bought it at a discount. But what do you think? They haven't developed production, and now they're selling us to the Arabs. At a profit. I can't bear to think what the Arabs will do to us. And our prime minister goes off to see Merkel, and never says a word to her about the shipyards."

"So the Germans are to blame for your problems?"

"And how! They brought the euro here so they could come on cheap holidays."

"You've received a lot of help from the European Union."

"Because once a German does come on holiday, he has to have everything like in Germany. They've built highways, they've restored the old sites. They've been trying to make it into a second Germany. But it won't succeed. Do you know what a German really is?"

I think I know, but I decide not to answer.

"The German is a robot. He gets up at six, goes to work, and gets drunk on schedule, once a week. And do you know what a Greek is? A Greek is good fun, friends, family. After work I always meet up with my friends. We sit and chat. We visit each other. But the German—I've read about it in the papers—never enters his neighbors' house. If I wanted to be a German, I'd dye my hair blond and start getting up at six. But I don't want to. So why don't they finally get lost and leave our economy alone?!"

There has to be a receipt

"German-style capitalism is already over for us. But the whole crisis started with it," says Loukas, an agency journalist. "In the past, I'd get a call five times a day from some bank or other offering me a nice little loan or a nice line of credit. That's not normal. But now? They never ring at all. They know that people have been hit in the wallet. I work for a state news agency, so they've cut my salary by 25 percent. My wife works for a private newspaper, and they've cut hers too. Many employers are taking advantage of the situation to fire people or to lower their salaries. There's no question of taking a vacation this year. It's a pity, because the kids have just gone off on their own, and we wanted to see Thailand.

"The government is trying to persuade us to get receipts or invoices for everything. It's estimated that the gray economy in our country may account for as much as 50 percent of the budget. Greece is known as a poor country of rich people.

"Receipts are all right, though at first the taxi drivers and doctors kicked up a bit of a fuss. I support all the changes—I see no alternative. But last week the full-blooded Greek in me came out. Our front door lock broke, so my wife and I decided to invest in a good, burglarproof replacement. The locksmith came and said, 'The lock will cost one hundred euros, and if you want a guarantee for it, you'll have to accept a receipt. My labor will cost another hundred—if you don't want a receipt. With a receipt it'll be one hundred twenty.'

"Of course I asked for him to do the work without a receipt, just like at the repair shop, the dentist's, and even the gas station. Lately, the government came up with the idea of giving tax inspectors the power to look in people's bags and ask them to show a receipt for any items they've bought. If they don't have one, they'll get a fine, and so will the storekeeper.

"I think that's going a bit too far. Like with the salary cuts. I can understand that for a few years we frittered our money away, and now we have to tighten our belts, but the cuts are too big. But we won't find out what the government is really up to until July. By then there'll be a hundred-degree heat wave, and whatever they do nobody will have the strength to protest."

Thursday, or storekeepers versus the euro

How do things look from the storekeepers' point of view? I ask Giorgos Burbulis, also known as Jurek, the Polish version of his name. Burbulis was the assistant to Kazimierz Górski, Poland's former national soccer team coach, in the days when he successfully coached several of the Greek clubs. Now Jurek is the owner of three Polish stores. A can of Łomża beer costs €1.00 at Jurek's stores. Raspberry syrup is €2.35. A can of "army" goulash is €3.40, and half a pound of smoked ham is €7.20. "But when you Poles enter the euro zone, I'll wind up the business. Because Poland is only competitive now. Even the Greeks buy Polish cooked meats from me, because they're good, and they cost less than the Greek ones. Of course everyone gets a receipt, without exception."

"All right, but how did a Greek come to run Polish stores?"

"During the war, in Greece, just as in Poland, the Home Army (with allegiance to the old, prewar government) and the People's Army (with allegiance to the future, postwar Communist government) fought against fascism. In Poland the People's Army won. But in Greece it was the Home Army. The ones who were on the Communist side, like my father for instance, were persecuted. My dad fled from Greece and ended up in Poland. That's where he met my mom. And that's where my brother and I were born."

Jurek's family came back to Greece in 1974, as soon as the dictatorship of the colonels ended. "We were one of the first families to return. My dad had never wanted to live anywhere else. He loved this country. I understood that many years later, when I myself came home from emigration—I spent twenty years living in the United States. Here the air is good, the food is good, and the people are good. Paradise! Anyway, take a look at my customers. They arrived here fifteen years ago and they don't want to go home at all."

His customers are Robert, Grzesiek, and Zdzich—all from Poland. They're drinking Łomża beer and praising Greece to the skies.

"Here if you have a beer and then drive a car, the cops just smile. They have a human approach," says Robert. "But in Poland I've heard you can go to jail. So why go back there?"

"Just don't write that we do nothing here but drink beer. If that were true, nobody would keep their job for long. We've been here for more than ten years, and we're still getting work. What's it like? Now that Poland is in the European Union, it's really good. We can work legally and nobody bothers us. Because before we joined, the police used to make raids on the building sites. If they caught you working illegally, you had to slip them some cash straightaway. Otherwise you were deported."

"And to get work legally you had to slip them some cash too."

"And to get their social security number."

"And to go see the doctor."

"So do you know why there's this crisis in Greece?" asks Jurek. "Everyone wants too much for himself. I'm not feeling it personally yet. But I can already see that the customers have stopped buying ham in three-ounce amounts. They've started buying it by the slice."

Friday, or lefties versus the state

Exarcheia is a district full of anarchists, Communists, Trotskyites, alter-globalists, and environmentalists. It's hard to find a patch of wall here that's free of graffiti. At the local cafés, the politicized youth spend all day and night debating how to change the world.

The police don't venture in here. At the very sight of them, stones start to fly. On weekends, officers with plastic shields are posted as a precaution at the main points in and out of Exarcheia. Occasionally, everyone at the café tables suddenly starts to sneeze.

"Tear gas. Our guys must be chasing around with the pigs some-where," the waiter then explains, and fetches some moistened handkerchiefs.

So I'm off to Exarcheia with a knot in my stomach. I start at a cozy square outside the polytechnic.

"Exarcheia? There are changes being initiated here that will reshape the whole of Greece, and if it all goes to plan, the whole world too," enthuses Maria, an architecture student. "One government has already fallen here—the colonels' junta. On November 17, 1973, the students at my polytechnic declared a strike. The citizens of Athens soon joined in with them, because they'd had enough of the dictatorship. The colonels got scared. They sent a tank to the college. Twenty-four people were killed. But that was how the changes began, thanks to which a year later we had a democratically elected government instead of the colonels."

The second time Exarcheia rebelled was in 2009. "The smart-est minds couldn't see it coming," says Maria. "It began when the police shot a young guy called Alexandros, who'd mouthed off at them. The whole of Exarcheia erupted. Soon after, the whole of Greece erupted too. People fought with the police, and every day there were riots, tear gas, and demonstrations. Several police sta-tions all over the country went up in flames."

They were the biggest riots since 1973.

Christos is a teacher at the nearby high school. "I've been working with the young people here for fifteen years. I was sure something like this would happen. The kids spend hours studying hard. They finish school. Then they go to college. But if I ask my former students what their ambitions are, they say they want a job in the state sector. Is it normal for a twenty-year-old to aspire to a job as a civil servant? Earning one thousand euros a month? But that's how it is in Greece. Because we don't manufacture anything. You can either work for the state or in tourism."

"But what does that have to do with the riots?" I ask.

"There's only work for the chosen few. You have to have contacts, and pay a bribe too. Then you have heaven on earth: bonus pay, and they can't throw you out. But for most students there's no future in Greece."

I ask Maria what it's like for young architects. "There are two state-owned firms that take on the most talented or better placed people—the ones who have a father or mother in the sector. Apart from that, there are a few private companies. But they rarely employ anyone. The choice? You graduate, and either you go abroad or you find work that's below your abilities. At a gas station or an office. If you're lucky, you get a job in tourism. I'm in my third year, and today I'm off to do an internship at one of the agencies that brings in tourists from Israel."

Maria takes me to the center of Exarcheia. The once attractive little square stinks of urine. "Hash? Coke? Something harder?" asks an immigrant from Africa as we enter the square. Those who didn't say no are trailing about the place. Someone's smoking a joint. Someone else is helping a pal to shoot up.

"Unfortunately, this place is getting more and more horrible," says Maria. "The city quite knowingly lets people do drugs here. When the foreign journalists come along, what do they see? Smackheads, grass that's been pissed on, graffiti. But Exarcheia is really about something totally different. It's about a refusal to accept capitalism. A rejection of the rat race. Here we're going to fight our way to victory."

"But what exactly are you fighting against? The crisis?" I ask. Maria waves a hand. "The crisis is chicken feed. There's been more than one of them before. We're going to fight against capitalism. To show people that they don't have to have a villa with a swimming pool and a helicopter to be happy."

"So what do you want to change?"

"We want to do away with capitalism. And after that we'll see. You'll realize we're starting a landslide here that will engulf the entire world."

ACKNOWLEDGMENTS

This book could not have been written or published in English translation without the help of several dozen, perhaps more than a hundred people. Here I shall mention only the most important of them by name. Some have helped me with this work in particular; others have believed in me and supported me with their advice and friendship since I first began to write; yet others taught me to write.

Agora Publishing, Mariusz Burchart, the Four Paws Foundation, Jadwiga Dąbrowska, Magdalena Dębowska, the editors of *Duży Format*, Anna Dziewit-Meller, Grzegorz Gauden, Paweł Goźliński, Dorota Górniak-Krumova, Zbigniew Jankowski, Izabella Kaluta, Krasimir Krumov, Antonia Lloyd-Jones, Marcin Meller, Izabela Meyza, Włodzimierz Nowak, Agnieszka Rasińska-Bóbr, Paulina Reiter, John Siciliano, Małgorzata Skowrońska, Mariusz Szczygieł, Mariusz Tkaczyk, Ewa Wieczorek, Ewa Wojciechowska, Albert Zawada, and Joanna Zgadzaj.

Thank you all, from the bottom of my heart.

My thanks are also due to the heroes of this book—from the Bulgarian bear keepers, via the custodians of the Stalin museum, to the car smugglers on the old Soviet border. For the time afforded me, for your trust, and for sharing your life stories with me—thank you.